THINKING POLITICALLY

THINKING
POLITICALLY

JEAN BLONDEL

WESTVIEW PRESS · BOULDER · COLORADO

Copyright © 1976 in London, England
by Jean Blondel

Published 1976 in the United Kingdom by
Wildwood House Ltd.

Published 1976 in the United States of America by
Westview Press, Inc.
1898 Flatiron Court
Boulder, Colorado 80301
Frederick A. Praeger, Publisher and Editorial Director

Printed and bound in Great Britain

Library of Congress Cataloging in Publication Data
Blondel, Jean, 1929–
    Thinking politically.

    Bibliography: p.
    1. Political science. I. Title.
JA66.B53 1975   320   75-38746
ISBN 0-89158-536-2

Contents

problem of functional equivalence. The end-products of structural theory: middle-range analyses; the study of political systems.

Accepting the diversity of political events with modesty. Being aware of underlying relationships in the maze of events. Being aware of the existence of distinct planes of analysis. Being aware of links between the branches of political analysis. Being aware of continuous and discrete elements in political life.

Preface

Every subject has its amateurs and its professionals, but perhaps in politics the gaps and misunderstandings between professionals and amateurs are larger than in any other field of human inquiry. Politicians and interested observers criticize political scientists for creating too much order out of what is in reality a mixture of habits, customs and uneasy compromises; they regard students of politics as unnecessary or dangerous, harmless or wasteful. Of course, politicians, observers and the man in the street are inconsistent: they ask professionals to draft constitutions, to account for election results, to explain military coups; while governments and political groups are more frequently – too frequently for some radicals – seeking the advice of professional political scientists. But the gap is still unnecessarily wide.

I hope that this little book will contribute to a better understanding of the aims of political science, its methods, problems and successes, as well as elucidating the internal contradictions and conflicts to which it is liable. I also hope that I may correct the illusion that political scientists are mere dreamers, by showing that one of their efforts is to comprehend the bizarre complexity of reality. Indeed, active politicians often have a more narrow outlook than they realize: their reality is limited to their immediate context, whereas the political scientist examines broader contexts.

Those who think politically are expected – particularly in times of crisis – to provide formulae for a better future; they have to guide and explain, for better and for worse. I shall try to give an unbiased account of this guidance and these explanations; hopefully the reader will then be able to make a more informed judgement of the varied panorama of interests, aims and subjects that political scientists choose. The subject is so varied, its substance so complex, that what is presented here should be seen – and hopefully will be seen – as only a preliminary introduction to the psychology and approaches of those who think politically. But if this book does give some insight into the profession of political science, much of the credit must belong to Robert Clower, of the Department of Economics of the University of California at Los Angeles (previously of Northwestern University and of the University of Essex) who urged me to try to give an account of the profession which has been mine all of my adult life: he has stimulated my thoughts and at times given me the courage to rise to this challenge. To him I am most indebted and grateful; though it is of course to me, and me alone, that mistakes, errors, undue silences or distorted judgments must be attributed.

J. BLONDEL

Mourillon, Toulon, France
July 1974

CHAPTER 1

Introduction

This book is about 'thinking politically'. It might be objected that 'politics' is commonly understood to be a somewhat shabby activity. How often has one heard people say 'these men are simply playing politics', when they refer to individuals who 'ought' to be idealistic instead of being concerned with their own careers, the dislodgement of others from positions, or some advantages for a little clique? For those who view politics in this way, 'thinking politically' can only be at best an attempt to discover rules about an activity which only exists because of the imperfections of men, and especially of rulers.

Politics does sometimes have a bad name. Yet even those who label politics as 'dirty' are often inconsistent in their attitudes. Few uniformly describe as 'dirty' all the political activities that they witness around them. 'Politicians' are normally denigrated, but 'statesmen' are viewed with respect. Those who would generalize about the character of politicians from corruption in some large cities admire a Roosevelt, a Churchill, a Gandhi, a Lenin or a Mao tse Tung. Few of those who wholly 'detest' politics are likely to read this book, but some might at least glance at its first page: so I ask you, would you definitely swear that politics is totally unredeemed? Have you never uttered a word of praise or felt any admiration for a politician? Do you believe that political activity can never achieve any worthwhile objective? Perhaps these attacks against politicians result from limited observations, not from a general appraisal.

But another group of critics – possibly more sophisticated and knowledgeable – argue that political activity does not lead to thinking, in the strong sense of the word, since politics cannot really be analysed systematically. Politics covers the behaviour

of millions of people in countless situations; chess is difficult
enough, yet it relates to a limited number of figures which can
only execute the moves that they are asked to do. In politics, men
are driven, led or followed in such different types of conditions
that the idea of 'thinking' about them, in a constructive, coherent and scientific manner seems to many to be impossible.
Politicians seem to have a 'flair' for what will succeed. They
often make mistakes, but they have their ear to the ground: they
sense the problems sufficiently accurately to be able, sometimes,
to correct their errors and succeed after all. 'Thinking politically' seems to relate to something more conscious and more systematic. Can it really be done?

I.   *Why 'thinking politically' may seem impossible*
While moral objections to the *whole* of politics can be fairly
easily dismissed, objections to the idea of politics as the subject
of coherent studies need to be considered carefully. Indeed,
periodically, doubts have been expressed – among intellectuals
as well as among laymen – about the very possibility of political
science. Admittedly, the subject has attracted thinkers, including
many of the best thinkers that the world, at least the Western
World, has known in the last 2,500 years. From Plato and
Aristotle to the twentieth century, nearly every generation has
produced writers who have tried their luck at studying politics,
at giving advice to politicians, at proposing blueprints for a
better society. In the last seventy years, and in particular since
the Second World War, the academic discipline of politics has
become established as a major subject of teaching and research,
in universities, colleges and many other centres. This has happened in Western Europe, in Eastern Europe and parts of the
Third World; in the United States the profession of political
science has even achieved real recognition. Though the discipline does not absorb resources on the scale of the natural
sciences, and though it may not attract as much attention as
economics and sociology in administrative and journalistic
circles, it has gained in strength and grown in stature and the
time may soon come when its acceptance will be universal or
near-universal: economics, after all, was barely recognized by
governments before Keynes; it was rarely taken seriously before
the First World War.

Yet, even though the subject has grown, even though it might be argued that slowly, but inexorably, the techniques of the discipline are becoming more rigorous, critics can still point to difficulties within the subject itself, and to strong differences of opinion between the professionals. Recent developments have not prevented many outsiders from levelling the same criticism as in the past: is there a coherent body of thought in the discipline of political science?

The model of economics might appear to show the direction in which political science should go, but for inherent irreconcilable differences between the two subjects. Economics has a well-defined object and clearly measurable instruments. It studies exchanges of goods and services; these can normally be priced, or at least they can be compared by using quantifiable units. On the other hand, economists can *postulate* that all things have a price and thus bring all the objects of their inquiry within the same framework; but the economists' postulate is open to attack: the 'value' of goods and services should not perhaps be measured by their current price. Similarly, the Euclidean postulate in mathematics, which states that only one line can be drawn through a point such that it is parallel to another line, could be set aside, and has indeed been set aside, despite its practical consequences in geometry, architecture and engineering: those who wanted to set up a new geometry have preferred to adopt other postulates.

In fact postulates are never either true or false; whether in mathematics, physics or economics, postulates are only a useful basis on which to build theories which help to understand our environment. Sometimes other postulates will seem more useful. The economists' postulate – that goods and services have a value which can be measured by price – is not really true; but it does help in understanding many transactions in modern societies, where money is a very common yardstick for goods and services.

Explanatory theories are built on these postulates: they are thus extremely important for the development of science. This is precisely where, unlike economics, political science seems to be deficient. Though it may be able to describe political events, it does not seem able to provide a straightforward and simple base – a postulate – on which to peg a long chain of reasoning.

Postulates such as the Euclidean postulate or the price postulate have given to geometry and economics their unity: goals are clear; the problems are circumscribed; the methodology can be discovered. On the contrary, the study of politics seems more amorphous, more eclectic in its aims, more slippery in its techniques of investigation.

To highlight the contrast, let us draw another example from economics: there are huge differences between family economics and national income budgeting: dollars, pounds, francs or yens mean really different things in different situations. There is even a sense in which these units have no concrete meaning; they are mere concepts in many calculations. An individual's capital may, in most circumstances, be easily realized, that is, turned into any amount of goods and services which this capital will buy; the same cannot be said of the huge assets of a State, or even a large company. But the same modes of thinking can be used for the individual, the company or the State. Exchanges of goods or services will or will not take place; the instrument of exchange will be the same form of currency, which is measurable. Granted that a nation cannot, and in effect does not, realize its assets, the exchanges which this nation's government concludes can still be analysed adequately by reference to a process which is not basically different from that which is applied to small firms or individuals. A general analysis can therefore proceed.

The same cannot be said for politics, where we are confronted with events, institutions and standpoints which cannot easily be compared against a single yardstick. Suppose you wanted to know what was necessary to understand activities in the American Senate. You would have to study various institutions, such as the party system, executive-legislative relations, grass-roots organizations. You would need to inquire into ideologies and myths in the American Republic. You would have to examine the careers and ambitions of politicians. Yet once that study was done, it would be of relatively little use if you then wished to inquire into the British House of Lords, the Japanese House of Councillors or the Ethiopian Senate. You would need to acquire for the United Kingdom, Japan or Ethiopia a knowledge similar to that which you acquired for the United States. Yet there is some connection between the American Senate and these other bodies; they are all second chambers and should have common features; indeed they are likely to have more common features than any two randomly selected political institutions, such as the American Democratic Party and the Soviet High Command. Second chambers are difficult to compare because the *yardstick* by which to compare them is far from apparent. If they were economic institutions, they could be compared by their turnover, their profitability, their rate of growth. If they were triangles or other geometric figures, they would be compared by the size of their angles or the length of their sides. These comparisons would lead to precise measurements; they would also relate those objects to all neighbouring objects studied in the discipline. In political studies, this just cannot be done. We seem confronted with a maze of unconnected events, institutions and ideas. We have central and local governments; we may, or may not, have political parties and elections: these elections may, or may not, be free; there may, or may not, be a free press and other communication media; the country may be liberal or socialist, oligarchical or democratic; it may be an open society or a dictatorship. How can all these be related through a single yardstick?

The study of politics covers a wider and more diffuse area of man's life than economics. This is why many – both specialists in the field and outsiders – have said that imagination and intuition play a large part in political analysis and always will do so alongside logic and 'science'. This is why the study of political matters has seemingly to be guided by events, by a close knowledge of history and of the special conditions of individual societies, by a careful examination of groups as well as a precise understanding of the motivation of 'great men', by an appreciation of the aspirations and ideals, as well as the selfishness, of mankind. The field is so diverse that some feel that no approach is specifically political. One has to borrow tools and techniques from many disciplines: some students of politics may be nearer to students of other disciplines than to other students of politics. When examining the politics of a tribal society, be an anthropologist! When examining small groups in committees, be a social psychologist! When assessing the role of a king or of a president, be a psychologist and an historian! When comparing the costs of engaging in international negotiations which might

lead to war with the welfare of minorities, be an economist! If
this is how one must exhort a student of politics, what can it
mean precisely to 'think politically'?

II.   *What thinking politically could mean, in an eclectic discipline*
Though there may be less unity in the study of politics than in
economics, physics or other sciences, is there no unity at all?
There may not be a postulate enabling political scientists to link
closely all the events that they wish to study. But even if the
types of inquiries are very diverse, there *is* a discipline; political
scientists do, in a broad fashion, recognize each other. Even if
they oppose each other, they use a language which has common
features. Economics may be tightly knit; the economists' price
postulate may be easily recognizable by all, insiders and outsiders alike. But is such a tightly organized structure an absolute
necessity for any discipline? Suppose that thinking politically
had some of the characteristics of tightrope walking, with the
constant danger that one might fall on one side or the other:
thinking politically would be more like a juggling act, but the
study would still be characterized by a profound unity.

Let us explore this point further. Underneath the objective
and practical unity which a common yardstick may give to a
discipline, unity can also come from a less precise common
thinking, from a sensitivity or alertness to problems: this helps
gradually to relate events, situations and descriptions to a
subject-matter. But here we seem caught in a vicious circle, as
this subject-matter may in fact only be defined out of the questions that come to be studied. Since there is no unity arising from
an obvious yardstick, the questions will be the loosely related
problems which appear to be interesting to curious observers.
Only accidentally will these problems become connected, if
they are connected at all.

This is true, but the predicament is perhaps not confined to
political science. The natural sciences appear now to have a
unified body of knowledge through the complex theory which
they have come to build; so has economics, at least to a degree.
But this is only the end-product of a long development:
geometry began from the desire to make measurements of the
earth; physics was long associated with the solution of various
discrete questions of gravitation, light and electricity. Similarly,

in its early stages, politics was concerned for instance with formulating the best constitution, without giving much consideration to an underlying general theme linking all the questions of
political life. Nor is it surprising that those who are interested in
politics come to the discipline because they are curious about
abstentions in local elections, participation among the citizen-
ship, the development of military rule in many parts of the
world, party discipline in legislative assemblies, the role of a
president in the passing of a bill, career patterns of leaders, or the
real meaning of concepts such as liberty, democracy and justice.

These questions are separate and discrete. They seem to
confirm the view that politics is extremely eclectic, that it covers
problems of broad extent. Yet, in the midst of these many problems, the question of unity recurs because, though many questions are studied, not all human problems come under the
searching eye of students of politics. A second phase has therefore to come, in the study of politics as in other disciplines. Problems need to be related by the determination of an *abstract*
subject-matter linking the many aspects which come to be studied. Students of politics never look at more than *some* of the
facts which come to their attention; they select, but they can
only do so because they are guided by a 'selecting' mechanism. If
one is interested in legislators as political actors, for instance,
one is not (at least not usually) interested in their dress, their
blood pressure, or their looks: one wishes to analyse their political characteristics. These have to be defined, at least in some
fashion; the political element in the attitudes and behaviour of
legislators has to be extracted. But, then, one is demonstrating –
if only unconsciously – a concern for a particular *type* of problem, a recognition of the kind of questions that are political.
One may not precisely define these problems; one may not be
able to find a 'unifying postulate'. But there has to be some
unity; there has ultimately to be some concept, idea, or at least
theme, which will be recurring in all the studies. The 'theme'
may be much looser than equivalent themes in economics. It
may be as vague as a description of sets of cases as is the phrase
which defines politics as being the 'study of men related to
authority'.[1] Some types of problems, and only some, come

[1] D. A. Strickland, L. L. Wade and R. E. Johnston, *A Primer of Political Analysis*
(Markham, Chicago, 1968), p.1.

nonetheless to be studied.

We can therefore say with assurance that thinking politically at least consists in looking at some events, questions or situations in ways which are related by a concern for a more abstract subject-matter, which we will need to define further: this might be authority, or it might be another concept. But, because one has to distinguish what is political from what is not, this process of selection necessarily provides some unity to the field of study. Of course, there will be room for disagreement about the importance of the questions chosen; of course, there will be different approaches. Some may say that it is more useful to study the relationship between big business and government than to examine the motivations of electors, on the grounds that more of politics is explained by questions of power at the top than by voting results. Others may not agree. But they will agree about some configuration for the subject-matter. Students of politics will extract 'political deposits' out of reality, though they may somewhat differ about the richness of the finds.

The existence of a discipline implies abstracting certain elements; it also implies a methodology. By methodology, one does not mean a technique, but an analytical process of defining problems, setting their limits, and finding some means of relating these problems to others already solved. Methods can range from intellectual tools, such as the use of logic, to more concrete procedures, such as practical experiments. A common methodology consists in choosing the documents which need to be studied, in abstracting the facts which need to be examined, as well as in selecting the tools which will be most effective in the analysis of either documents or facts. Method even means a feel for what is practical within the limitations of both time and money.

Methodology is linked to and derives from subject-matter. The methodology may not be simple, easy to handle, or even always successful: problems are often hard to seize, at times even insoluble. But this is not uncommon in other sciences. Political scientists are able to assess what is insoluble or at least difficult, given the various techniques which are at their disposal. This is perhaps the main point of a methodology. Students of politics sense that they can only describe inadequately, rather than define, certain complex problems; they may know that they can only find unsatisfactory substitutes (indicators of a concept rather than the concept itself) or make certain assumptions which are highly, or at best somewhat, unrealistic. Think of concepts such as justice, power or democracy: can definitions of them be easily given, or – even more – applied to a large number of concrete situations? Political activity is extremely varied; the subject-matter extremely diffuse and eclectic; it should not be surprising that the 'methodological baggage' of political scientists has to include scepticism and critical analyses as well as 'forward leaps', suspicions and doubts about broad concepts as well as longings for, and even occasionally naïve collapses into, over-hasty generalizations.

The intractable nature of the subject therefore leads naturally to conflicting approaches. Battles between the various schools of thought – between quantifiers and describers, between empiricists and systematizers of the most abstract character – may seem to outsiders (and sometimes to insiders) an indication of the lack of coherence of the discipline; they may even give the impression that the problems will never be satisfactorily solved.[2] But this does not mean that there is no unity behind the differences, no methodology behind these many approaches (part of the methodology being precisely an awareness that the subject-matter has to be considered in an eclectic way). Political problems, due to their diffuseness and amorphousness, are difficult to grasp. The eclecticism of the subject-matter leads to an eclecticism of the methodology, and as one cannot expect any political scientist to share more than in part in this eclecticism, it is the whole profession of political science which must by its breadth and variety provide the subject with the eclecticism it needs.

In our attempt to appreciate 'thinking politically', then, we have established that it is an eclectic form of thinking. It proceeds partly from forms of thinking which prevail in other disciplines: an uneasy balance between the various approaches results. We can now at least see the lines which our inquiry

[2] See for instance R. C. Macridis, *The Study of Comparative Government* (Random House, New York, 1955), *passim* (primarily in relation to comparative politics); more generally, D. Easton, *The Political System* (Knopf, New York, 1953), ch. 2, pp. 38-63.

should take. First, we need to discover the scope of political
inquiry and the approaches that characterize the study of
politics. Second, we have to find behind these approaches the
common concern that links students of politics to their
subject-matter. Third, we must look at the methods which are
used and see how political scientists relate their inquiries to the
subject-matter.

We shall then be able to return to the approaches and see, in
the second part of this book, what differences and also what
similarities there are between the methods and treatment of
subject-matter. As we shall see in the next chapter, norms,
structures and behaviour are the three broad divisions on which
we need to concentrate. We shall therefore try to see how thinking politically contributes in a significant fashion, alongside
disciplines which are neater, simpler and more respectable, but
not more important, to answering those questions that, from
curiosity or necessity, mankind has incessantly raised and wished to solve.

PART I

*The General Aspects of
Political Thinking*

CHAPTER 2

The many approaches to politics

The best way to conduct our inquiry into the boundaries, subject-matter and methods of political thinking is to start by describing the panorama of approaches of political scientists. It might be intellectually more satisfying to proceed deductively, by first giving a comprehensive definition of the scope of political inquiry and thereby discovering the various fields of analysis and the various segments of the discipline. But the richness and breadth of political inquiry suggest that we proceed differently and cast our net as widely as possible over the many varieties of political scientists before examining how the different approaches can be united. If there is a common concern in the discipline (a matter to be discussed in the next chapter), it will only become apparent when we know what all scholars do and what they aim to do. Let us therefore give an impression of the controversies which have arisen in the past and still arise at present. This examination cannot be exhaustive in so short a book; but it will help to give more content to our assessment of the nature of political thinking.

A glance at the history of political analysis reveals three main battlefields. One is the opposition between unique events and generalizations and raises indirectly the question of 'quantification'. Another is the opposition between legalism and the factual or realistic presentation of happenings. And in the third 'descriptive' confront 'normative' studies which have recently made a strong comeback: they were one of the main objects of political analysis in the past, but were relegated to second place in the postwar period.

I. *The unique and the general*
During the recent period, one controversy seemed to dominate

the field of political science. Under the name of 'behaviourism', first in the United States, and later in Europe, the discipline underwent a major change. A battle of 'the Ancients and the Moderns' took place. The 'Moderns' propounded the need for rigour, for systematization, and, perhaps above all, for quantification. In increasingly large numbers, those who believed in the role primarily of statistics, but also of mathematics as a whole in political analysis suggested that without such tools political science would never come to achieve 'true' scientific status.[1] Meanwhile, the 'Ancients' remained committed to a more descriptive and less systematic analysis, often based on the examination of isolated historical events.

Yet the battle over quantification is only a symbol of a wider issue: behind it lies the clash between those who believe that the discipline should concentrate on general problems and those who emphasize the role of the unique. Let us briefly consider the 'case' and the points which are argued.

A. *Quantification.* In the last few decades, quantification has been the main subject of the controversy. Those who argue for it suggest that there is a need to become more precise by trying to give numbers to the findings which are made. Instead of stating that 'some' British workers vote Labour and others Conservative, one should give percentages. Instead of saying that Prime Minister X had more influence on politics than Prime Minister Y, one should examine policies and assert precisely degrees of influence.

These two examples suggest both the case and the limitations or problems of the case. There is surely nothing wrong, quite the contrary, with the first example. It is better to know precisely the percentage of manual workers who vote Labour than to know this only vaguely. Moreover, not only do such figures provide a better equipment to describe situations: they also enable us to relate some descriptions to other descriptions – and gradually to

[1] The debate over behaviourism marked much of the 1950s and 1960s in the United States. The hope was that a behavioural approach, with its statistical and mathematical methods, would lead to more systematic analyses than an institutional approach. For an impression, see R. A. Dahl, 'The behavioural approach in political science', *American Political Science Review,* 55 (December 1961), pp. 763-72: and A. Ranney, ed., *Essays on the Behavioural Study of Politics* (University of Illinois Press, Illinois, 1962), *passim.*

produce theories. If we know the percentage of the Labour vote which is of the working class, we can examine its progress over time; if we know the percentage of Catholics in the Labour vote, we can also discover whether class or religion is more important in the Labour vote. Recent statistical techniques have improved and new tests have been shown to be useful in neighbouring social sciences: quantification, for instance, has increased its impact on economics, where mathematics has truly transformed the nature of most inquiries: it seems at first sight uncontroversial that political analysis would gain by following a similar path.

But the matter is uncontroversial, however, only in so far as figures come 'naturally' from the field of study. This is where the second example – about Prime Ministers – comes to suggest problems. In election studies there are votes, which can be counted; they come from men who are working class or not, Catholic or not. But there are other areas where figures do not emerge naturally. We can count votes but can we count influence? Can we express justice in numbers? Perhaps we can say that Prime Minister X was more influential than Prime Minister Y or that there was more justice in some actions than in others. But how do we quantify this 'more' or this 'less'? Hence the dilemma: if we believe that figures are necessary to increase precision, then we have to *create* figures, to impose numbers on situations where they do not emerge naturally from the field of study.

Of course, it may be said that numbers are also created in other situations. In economics, for instance, it is man and society, not nature, who have given a price to commodities. Prices express the preferences of consumers and producers, but they express those preferences that result from society as it is organized; each individual *assumes* these preferences as if they were a given, but prices are not really objective in the true sense of the word. Yet, because so many people agree that prices have a meaning, and indeed live by these prices, the economist can take prices as givens and play on differences as if they had an objective existence and had the same meaning for each individual. Students of politics rarely have such good fortune. They may treat election results as givens; but if they wish to assess attitudes to see whether a political party will gain or lose from policy choices in the future, they have to *engineer* figures because scales of preferences are not givens in the way prices are. When we prefer commodities, we express our preference in terms of price: we would pay more, for instance, for a television than for a pair of shoes. When we *feel* that we prefer Party A to Party B, or Leader X to Leader Y we have no similar method of comparison. In economics, there is an interpersonal and universal scale for goods and services, which people accept (though they may not always agree to this scale). In politics (except in the election field), scales have to be *contrived* from 'rank-orderings' which are not adopted naturally or automatically. There is no universal interpersonal scale, whether between attitudes to governments, likes and dislikes of committee members, preference for peace rather than butter, and choice of liberty rather than equality.

This is why even those who believe in quantification and are 'missionary' about numbers remain somewhat uneasy about their extensiveness. Quantifiers know that most of politics is not quanti*fied*; they have to recognize that most of politics is not even readily quanti*fiable*. They argue that the situation can be improved by a constant effort. The real contention between the two sides is over the quantifiers' belief that political analysis can only be improved by quantification because it provides the precision that the science requires. Quantification arises from the desire to give the inquiry a more general and scientific aspect.

Their argument is that a science must be based on numbers if it is to exist, an argument supported by the influence of mathematics in the natural sciences and economics. But what is the real foundation for such a discipline, if numbers do not emerge naturally when one studies, for example, justice or liberty, or personal likes and dislikes for rulers or policies? Despite the display of prejudice by some of the critics of quantification, despite the fact that, in some cases, anti-quantifiers refuse to look at these techniques, let alone use them whenever possible, the main point does remain: in many important areas of political thinking, quantification is at best very difficult and often impossible to use.

B. *The many variables.* The search for scientific precision is also made difficult by the vast complexity of many problems. Even where quantification is possible, as in elections, the large number of variables raises major difficulties: when looking for the possible 'causes' of voting behaviour, one can think of occupation, religion, ethnic background, parental origin, environment, party programmes, personality of candidates, and many other factors. In trying to predict how legislators are likely to behave on a number of issues, one must look at their past record on similar issues, at their network of friends, at the likely pressure from constituents, at the *perception* of these pressures by the legislators, and at the possible stands of the party leaders. There seems to be no end to the number of variables which have to be examined: the idea that scientific laws can be discovered about the behaviour of legislators or the votes of electors seems an impossible dream. Only by oversimplifying can conclusions be drawn; but are we entitled to oversimplify?

C. *The unique.* We have hitherto considered *general* types of influence on a situation, such as attitudes to parties or the relationship between legislators over various issues; but not all problems are general. Some events, such as a war, a *coup d'état,* even a major piece of legislation, appear to be 'unique'. Can these readily be reduced to 'classes' of broader events?

Unique events concern those who think politically in one of two main ways. First, politics is concerned with 'great men'. Economists can study economic forces; sociologists can deal with social problems; both can reduce great men to 'epiphenomena'. Political scientists cannot, because, however politics is defined, it must include decisions taken by public leaders, both collectively and singly. Some of these leaders have great reputations: these reputations have to be explained. The student of politics is concerned with the way decisions are taken and not just with sequences, movements or trends; at some point he is called upon to say why it was, in his view, that a particular government took a particular line, and what part a leader may or may not have played in a given process. For the students of other disciplines, this could be mere gossip, but for the student of politics, this is the stuff of his subject. If he cannot give an explanation, he has to recognize that it is his own, or the discipline's, failing, not a trivial matter which can be left aside.

Some students of politics may be driven to suggesting that great men do not count, or count very little. But this, too, has to be proved, and can only be proved by looking successively at the roles of great men; not only great men, but leaders of all types have to be studied by political scientists. Whether the American president is, or is not, great, the question remains of how much difference it makes if X, rather than Y, is president. And, to the chagrin of political scientists, government after government – in totally different contexts – shows a predilection for powerful leaders. The problem cannot be by-passed, though one may try to solve it by lumping leaders together, either in a particular country and ignoring the time element, or in a particular historical period and ignoring the regional element. But leaders remain scarce, and circumstances differ so much that comparisons are at best far-fetched. The problem of the unique in political science is not created by historians; rather, historians come to study politics because the study of the careers of unique men has a natural place in political science.

The second way in which the unique concerns those who think politically is in the examination of historical events; some of these are so important that they constitute landmarks in political life. One *has* to dissert on the causes of the French and Russian Revolutions: these are Events of the first order. But, though they may be explained, they cannot always be categorized. Of course, there have been other revolutions: but none have had the same impact, and many were offspring of these revolutions. 1789 and 1917 are unique. They were so momentous that they are studied now not only for their historical value but also for their influence on present-day politics.

The unique character of men and events thus gives a peculiar twist to political analysis – and in particular to the methods used in this analysis. Because of their undoubted importance in many decisions and in patterns of beliefs, great men and great events do not merely suggest that a place be given to historians and that students of politics be at least in part historically minded. They also suggest that discrete changes are important in themselves – indeed often more important than incremental and regular trends. Men and accidental events seem to produce sudden changes of direction in the 'curve' of history. Hence the view that general laws may determine the regularities of daily happenings, but that they may be much less momentous than the large accidents which may at times occur. By their very nature, these great accidents are unpredictable. So political science is always aware that miracles happen, and that predictions are always liable to their impact.

The conflict between the unique and general schools of thought runs through the whole of political science. The study of general trends is neither new nor restricted to a narrow group. The works of Aristotle, Machiavelli or Hobbes, to cite only a few, were truly general. There have always been political scientists who looked for general rules which they hoped to apply to all circumstances. What is new is the way in which mathematics has made large inroads in much of politics, partly because of the novelty of many mathematical techniques (statistics were discovered in the late eighteenth century and did not come of age before the late nineteenth), while many other methods used in political analysis (game theory is perhaps the most common) have been discovered in the last few decades. Only the calculus has been available for a very long period, but measurement problems have always limited its sphere of application in political studies. Due to the frequent occurrence of unique events in politics, there have always been objections to quantification.

Of course, students of unique events often exaggerate their case; anti-quantifiers have a habit of dismissing all quantitative discoveries, though it has repeatedly been shown that 'trivial' quantitative discoveries are much less trivial than critics have suggested.[2] The obsession with the unique can, and often does, lead to a love of anecdotes;[3] the possibility of 'epic' phenomena can lead to a rejection of predictive statements. But these exaggerations do not undermine the existence of *some* phenomena, at least as objects of study needing explanation.

It is both healthy and important that the eclecticism of students of politics should lead them at times to examine and describe in the most brute, empirical, non-formal manner events of magnitude and the lives of great men. Such studies are essential

[2] See P. F. Lazarsfeld, 'The American soldier, an expository review', *Public Opinion Quarterly* (Fall 1949), pp. 377-404; in particular the early part, in which the author gives examples of a number of findings which run directly against what would have been normally expected in relation to the characteristics of American soldiers.

[3] This was precisely the reason why the behavioural approach developed: unless points are related to a general theory, what is the point of narrating, for instance, the history of a particular American president?

even if they result in giving an exaggerated place to some facts and if there is, as a result, a waste of energy. The approach – historical, poetic or artistic – to unique happenings forces students of politics to look at reality. Politicians criticize political scientists for being too abstract and for not understanding all the implications and all the reasons for the developments in which they are involved. Those students of politics who look at these events may not always improve our scientific knowledge of political life, but they ensure that the influence of an event or a statesman is not underestimated. They will have a place for as long as quantification raises serious problems in the analysis of political reality.

II.   *Law and reality. The problem of structures*
The question of reality – and, as its corollary, the role of history – affects in another way those who think politically. Just as the controversies over quantification relate to the more basic question of a general analysis, so attacks on the formal character of the legal approach are related to the basic question of 'realism'. The argument against the legal approach is that political science should be concerned with what is, rather than with what the law proclaims; that, particularly over the last twenty years, the legal approach has hindered political analysis by dissecting constitutional texts and neglecting to consider their effectiveness; that too much has been written on the formal powers of assemblies and courts when reality shows these bodies to be subservient to governments. The stress on a legal approach which is evident in political studies is often explained in terms of the number of lawyers in the academic profession of politics, which is felt to be too large. While historians played a large part in the development of the discipline in some centres (principally in Britain, alongside philosophers), lawyers had a major influence elsewhere: to the present day in many Continental countries political science is linked with legal studies. The most common bond is constitutional law: though other branches of public law, in particular administrative law where, as in France, the tradition is strong, have often been at the origin of political studies.

Lawyers are unquestionably over-concerned with formal institutions; the criticisms levelled against them have much justification. But it is important to see why legal studies have played a large part in political analysis: reality, though not wholly governed by formal rules, is moulded by them to a large extent. Formal rules often constrain and therefore influence behaviour. The problem rotates around the question of implementation of rules, and the role which the notion of rules plays in political life.

A. *The problem of implementation.* Since many laws are not applied or at best ill applied, why concentrate on the study of laws? To answer this question, we need first to decide what implementation means. Is a law implemented when government officials strive to apply the law? This is not sufficient, since these government officials may simply not be obeyed. Nor can we say, at the opposite extreme, that the law is implemented only when universally obeyed: no law would ever meet such a requirement. Perhaps an accepted definition is that a law is implemented if 'on the whole' people tend to obey it. But even this laxer definition needs to be qualified. Laws are often complex: they are becoming increasingly complex and increasingly numerous. They are sometimes contradictory; they leave scope for interpretation; the 'spirit' of the law may be at variance with the 'letter'; implementation is not mechanical or automatic. Technical problems have to be solved to see what form of words will achieve the desired result, and if one can be devised to do it better. Whether acting politically or thinking politically, one is constantly reminded of the limitations of all rules; the problem of implementation is always present.

Thus it is too easy to say that legal documents, constitutions for instance, are not implemented. Anti-Soviet writers often suggest that the Soviet Constitution of 1936 exists on paper only and therefore need not be seriously examined. Realists tend to pooh-pooh efforts at examining the rules contained in this document. But is that constitution really not implemented at all? Does practice at no point take account of the constitution? Is only the letter of the constitution applied while the spirit of the most important points is flouted? How does one isolate these most important points? Surely the constitution is applied in part, that part varying at different times? The question of partial implementation can refer both to the extent to which the laws are intended to be enforced and to the extent to which they are observed – either due to ignorance of the law or to deliberate disobedience. One has only to think of traffic laws to see the many dimensions which the problem can take. So one needs to examine in detail the relationship between law and reality.

There are other considerations: one could measure the degree of implementation of different laws; one could make such measurements at different moments; one would then see that degrees of implementation of the various laws can vary appreciably over long time periods. Laws may be introduced to change behaviour, but this is never achieved immediately. It always takes at least some time for elites and the public to adjust to the law. It is therefore not realistic to assume that laws will be implemented from the very moment when they are introduced: partial implementation is an endemic – though varying – factor in the administration of laws, as all governments know, who create law enforcement agencies to cope with the problem. This means, however, that, for students of politics, law and reality, rules and practice, are linked together in a permanent and complex fashion.

The problem arises if we want to analyse reality; it arises also if we want to improve it. It therefore arises at the very moment we begin to think of new laws if we are discontented with the reality. New laws are proclaimed because of an assumed need to redress an existing situation, either because laws currently in force are held to be unjust, or because people have adopted habits which are thought to be wrong. New laws aim to change, not just rules, but modes of political, social and economic behaviour. The procedure may be clumsy, but it is viewed consciously or felt unconsciously to be an instrument of change. Yet what we saw earlier implies that new laws must not demand too rapid or too extensive a change in people's habits, or the law will 'skid', so to speak: the population will ignore it while law enforcement agencies armed with strong powers will both be required and be ineffective. There is a maximum 'distance' between current habits and what the law can ask for. Beyond a point, implementation will be so rare, so difficult, so costly in terms of police and administration, that it seems unrealistic to force the experiment. The 'returns' for the government might indeed be smaller than the 'tension' incurred.

Since problems of partial implementation of laws, or degrees of implementation over time, of maximum 'distance' between new provisions and current reality are among the most serious questions of political life, it is just not sufficient for students of politics to look at behaviour; they need to examine the way in which laws are drafted and thus become, at least in part, lawyers. Of course, such analyses of 'distance' are still likely to be vague – unquantifiable! Often only experience will suggest whether populations will accept a new law and whether implementation will tend to increase in time. But lawyers can at least suggest which documents will be easier to understand, or be less ambiguous; they might show that some goals may not easily be applied and turned into specific forms of words. Lawyers thus remind realists of the role of new rules: those who think politically just cannot ignore the lessons which they teach.

B. *The problem of structures*. But perhaps we do not need 'lawyers' laws; perhaps change can be effected by different means. Some 'radical' nations, China or Cuba for instance, seem to want to change attitudes through modes of 'socialization' or 'cultural revolutions', instead of through laws as the West has known them. Legal documents may be suited primarily to some types of societies, liberal societies in particular, in which governmental action has tended to conform to fairly rigid procedures. Is the legal method merely one formula in order to introduce change, just as the stock exchange is one device out of many which attract investment? Might not a political system operate without laws?

'Lawyers' laws, statutes and constitutions – defined as written documents adopted according to a pre-defined procedure – are not universal. Not all countries have constitutions; indeed, until fairly recently, very few countries had such written basic rules. But, though all States may not live with laws and constitutions, they all live by some *rules*. These rules may not be 'made' according to formal procedures; but there will be customs. These customs specify, often as precisely as laws, what members of the polity are or are not to do. They control or direct behaviour in the same way as laws. And while we may not find everywhere formal legal documents, we find these rules, these *structures,* do exist everywhere: they are the underlying basis of families, tribes, associations, governments and of procedures, such as the pre-eminence of elders, the strength of precedents,

majority rule. The origins of these structures and procedures are
diverse; their forms are varied. But some structures and some
procedures pattern everywhere the behaviour of men.

These structures are often called institutions, partly to
distinguish them from procedures, which are also methods of
guiding behaviour. The family is an institution: it establishes
relations between certain individuals; in families, there are
procedures, for instance, establishing who is to make decisions
and on what basis the decisions are to be made. Indeed, there is
no real difference between institutions and procedures, as institutions are sets of procedures. A political party is an institution:
it is also a set of procedures by which leaders are chosen, decisions are taken, election campaigns are organized. It regulates
behaviour, as members of the party are expected to react in
certain ways. This happens in all aspects of political life. Tribes
and pressure groups, parties and bureaucracies, legislatures and
courts, all regulate behaviour by customs or 'lawyers' laws, indeed often by both. This is true in 'radical' countries and in
conservative politics, in authoritarian States and in liberal
systems. Whether Mao's China or Castro's Cuba have laws or
not, behaviour is patterned by institutions and procedures;
indeed, as the leaders of these countries wished to replace past
habits, institutions and procedures by new ones, they tended to
impose these new rules by a variety of means.

The universal existence of these structures gives a peculiar
complexion to political thinking. Political scientists cannot just
look at reality: they have to look at the means by which reality is
changed. They have continuously to refer both to structures and
behaviour. It is the legalists' function to show the importance
and limits or rules in the dynamic development of political life.
Legalism in political science is thus here to stay: its role is critical
if, in the deepest sense, studies of politics are to give a realistic
account of the whole of political behaviour.

Yet legalism is also important in another sense. Lawyers'
laws, as we said, tend to lay emphasis on the regular fashion in
which rules come to change. This is often attacked by politicians
as it seems to overlook more rapid change and implies
agreement on some fundamentals. Liberal societies are guided
by the 'rule of law': behind this principle lies a normative view –
that we should not be forced to act unless we know in advance

what rules operate. But another – realistic – principle also comes into play: what if the rule of law made it easier for men to accept new rules? Maybe the rule of law implies more and slower procedures; but greater uncertainty about the change of rules may lead the citizens to more cynicism. While this may not be the case in all circumstances, the point is surely valid in some situations: procedures and methods of change are thus inextricably linked with extent and type of change.

Legalism is thus related to political thinking in a number of ways: first, laws are in fact a means by which change does occur, though problems of implementation inevitably arise. Second, legalism helps to focus on structures which organize and pattern every society. Third, legalism raises questions of regularity in the process of change. Studies of laws and rules thus force behaviourists to examine structures and discuss obedience. They show that the border between 'is' and 'ought' is at best unclear in political life and that realism just cannot be achieved if we merely concentrate on a description of successive happenings.

Yet the legalistic approach has had a further and no less pervasive influence on political thinking. By looking for principles and general rules, lawyers drew political science towards a general set of inquiries. The legal mind helped to devise and classify constitutional schemes: though many constitutional schemes have been ill-applied or half-implemented, the general approach to structures and procedures led political analysis towards the scientific rigour of general laws. It is no accident that one of the great classics of political science, the eighteenth-century writer Montesquieu, applied his *legal* mind to the discovery of laws of *social* behaviour and to the elaboration of a constitutional blueprint. Over 2,000 years before him, Aristotle also looked for general arrangements in the constitutions of his time. Structures, procedures and laws provide a basis for generalizations. The legal approach is thus a crucial element in the vast, windy temple of political thinking.

III.   *Normative and descriptive political science*
While some of the classics of political science felt a need for generalizing on the basis of a legal approach, most felt even more strongly the need for moralizing. The two are indeed linked as we just began to see: constitutions and statutes are introduced

to bring about change, and changes are proposed on the basis of some norm held to be preferable to existing arrangements. This is why, not surprisingly, many rebelled against a descriptive view of political science: the claim has even been made that the function of the discipline is, on the contrary, to provide a critique of current situations and outline new principles to be implemented.

Yet for a period around 1960, normative political theory seemed in danger, if not of disappearing, at least of being reduced to a pious examination of great texts of the past, possibly on the grounds more of their literary and historical importance than of their relevance to modern conditions. Descriptive, scientific political science seemed on the verge of a breakthrough, due to the behavioural revolution which was then gaining ground in the United States. Political scientists were called upon primarily to set up general hypotheses and to attempt to test these hypotheses through the use of statistical and mathematical techniques. Supporters and opponents of traditional political theory noted that, in contrast to the blossoming of behavioural works, significant normative studies had become rare – perhaps forgetting that 'great works' are always rare and that only our compressed view of history makes us consider Hobbes and Locke, or Rousseau and Burke as contemporaries conducting a great debate.[4] But the trend seemed to be away from examining values; it seemed to be in the direction of close analyses of political life through the use of increasingly refined techniques of studying reality.

The tide turned abruptly at the end of the 1960s, however, partly because some supporters of the behavioural approach noted a resurgence of interest in values in the world around them and partly because political science had become too narrow in the behavioural mould: the study of politics proved once more to be eclectic and broad. The truly positive reasons which militate, not just for the inclusion, but for a major role to be given to values came once more to the fore, sometimes with a

[4] Hobbes was born in 1588 and died in 1679; he wrote *Leviathan,* his main work, in 1651, while Locke (1632-1704) wrote his *Two Treatises on Civil Government* in 1690. Rousseau was born in 1712 and died in 1778; he wrote his main political work, *Social Contract,* in 1762, while Burke (1729-97) wrote his *Reflections on the Revolution in France* in 1790.

vengeance. Events which deeply affected the Western World, ranging from opposition to the Vietnam war in the U.S. to boredom and lack of real direction among intellectuals everywhere reduced the apparent importance of empirical or descriptive studies while leading to a return to the examination of the basic principles underlying society. This was further emphasized by an opposition to 'value-free science'; some suggested, indeed over-emphasized, that norms and values permeate all intellectual activity. Attempts were made to demonstrate that far from being an honest empirical attempt to examine the reality of politics, behaviourism was a machine designed to support the *status quo*: the instruments used to examine reality were held to be so biased that they led automatically to viewing present situations as good or inevitable.

When taken to extremes, these criticisms of descriptive political science are as 'mystical' as are exaggerated views about the role of great men or the role of constitutions. In the last resort only empirical work can show that empirical studies have the characteristics that critics claim they have! Yet political thinkers have often in the past been political philosophers, concerned with the discussion of values and goals of human societies. The prescriptive element has always been larger in the study of politics not only than in physics or other natural sciences, but than in economics, psychology and perhaps even sociology, at least parts of sociology. Prescriptive elements not only emerge at the level of discussions of overall goals or the building up of utopias; they also come into play when political scientists set up rules of conduct to guide politicians towards the resolution of the conflicts of goals with which they are confronted. Both these activities go beyond what is normally demanded of economics or physics, which are prescriptive only in a conditional sense.

A. *Technical or conditional prescription.* If a political scientist suggests that the executive in a parliamentary system will be stable only when one of the parties reaches about forty per cent of the national vote, he makes a prescriptive statement: but the prescription is conditional. The decision-makers have the option to decide whether or not to have a stable executive. Political scientists may add further that an unstable executive may prove ineffective in implementing policies, whether conservative or radical: this, too, is prescriptive, but remains conditional.

Those in power may still prefer a representative executive to an effective one. Such statements of course may not be correct, but whether correct or not, they are statements of a technically or *conditionally prescriptive character*; though they may induce a ruler to take a course of action, they do not directly advise him on the overall aims on which he is to act.

Conditionally prescriptive statements are the corollary and even the justification of empirical science; economists frequently make such statements. They are of the same order as statements made by physicists or biologists – they stem from the general principles of science. If A happens, B will (or will at least statistically tend to) happen. It was to discover relationships of this kind that behavioural political science felt the need for an increased use of quantitative techniques, though, as we saw earlier, the search for general relationships much preceded the use of quantitative techniques and dates back as far as Montesquieu and even Aristotle.

B. *Goals and utopias.* Technically prescriptive statements leave the decision-maker free to decide in one direction or the other: they merely warn of the consequences of any choice of action. But because the political thinker is concerned with politics in general, he cannot, as the economist or the engineer, restrict his advice to conditional prescription. Political parties decide on their programmes: political scientists are drawn to discuss the general goals as well as the details of political programmes. If these programmes wish to change society and bring about, for instance, greater equality or greater liberty, the political thinker will be drawn into a discussion of the intrinsic value of greater equality or greater liberty. Gradually, he becomes confronted with the 'eternal values' on the basis of which men make their fundamental choices.

There is almost no limit to this involvement: though theoretically the political scientist might not wish to concern himself with individual values, individual values lead to actions, and very few actions are without social implications.[5] Individual freedoms are never wholly individual: the various problems raised by the relationship between man and society under the label of liberty come therefore within the purview of political

[5] John Stuart Mill discussed these implications and formulated a distinction between self- and other-regarding actions in *On Liberty* (Chapter 4).

thinkers. So does the concept of equality, which is a social problem *par excellence,* and which cannot be conceived of in an individual context.

Goals such as equality and liberty need to be discussed carefully if political thinkers are to fulfil their role; political thinkers
have to argue a case and justify it on moral grounds. They have
to use logic to deduce a chain of consequences from an overall
principle. In an argument in favour of freedom of expression, for
example, an examination of the logical consequences of such a
stand would be an essential ingredient to convince an audience.
A moral commitment would have to be stated; for example
freedom of expression might be represented as a good in itself;
and this moral commitment would then be re-stated each time
difficulties emerged from the argument – for instance, the possibly dangerous consequences of extreme freedom of expression.
Political thinkers thus have to take sides, *unscientifically,* in favour
of freedom or in favour of a more organized – organic – State, in
favour of equality or of differences in status.

Such debates cannot be avoided: they are rightly viewed by
some as among the most important which mankind has to face.
Naturally enough, some students of politics, whether they are
called political philosophers or political scientists, must – and
will – be involved in the analysis of these problems. Political
thinkers have to be the 'imaginative' part of society, because
they have to 'invent' new goals for the society. They may make
impractical suggestions or appeal only to a small fraction of the
population: they may suggest a perfectly equal society, for instance, or in one which one 'ruler' decides for the benefit of all.
Yet both types of suggestions, which might not be universally
accepted, open up a new range of possibilities. It is therefore
literally true that ideas or goals are invented and afterwards
become part of the human political baggage. This 'invention' of
goals logically implies a lack of realism; yet society would be
more constrained if these goals were not discussed. Today's
impractical ideas become tomorrow's reality.

Utopias are the most elaborate and comprehensive end-
products of political analysis; they are depictions of ideal
human relationships in society. From Plato to Marx, and indeed
since Marx, utopia-building has been a common disease. The
polity has at times been conceived as an 'organism' with a head

and limbs, with each of the limbs having a specific and different function; or it has been conceived as a society of equals, where no one has the power to control the activities of others, the polity being organized as a confederacy of small communities. Since these utopias are pictures of a complete world, political thinking has, like philosophy or poetry, many of the characteristics of Sisyphus' effort. Utopia-building cannot develop in a linear fashion, using the findings of the past as steps for the future; it takes into account the previous efforts which have been made, but the process is not one of a gradual build-up. Yet it is almost as important for a political thinker to be imaginative as it is for a scientist trying to discover the truth to be systematic.

C. *Guidelines for action.* The search for a better life leads to a need for formulating overall goals and for elaborating utopias; this need lies behind normative thinking. General viewpoints then become translated into guidelines for action which attempt to solve conflicts of goals at a lower level. This is quite distinct from the conditionally prescriptive analysis that we described earlier: the point is not to discover the best way of achieving a goal while leaving to the decision-makers the responsibility to choose goals; it is rather to state explicitly where goals come in conflict and assess which goal is to be preferred in given circumstances. For example, assuming that individual freedom is a goal, it must be recognized that the freedom of an individual A should not encroach on the freedom of individual B. In the case of freedom of expression a limit must be set to decide what verbal attacks are slanderous, or how far the press should be allowed to publish lies or State secrets. Empirical analysis can give an answer if, say, the stability of the State is threatened; but an underlying choice must still be made between freedom of expression and the good of the State.

Those who think politically have thus to make a moral or idealistic case for one form of action rather than another. This is why guidelines are not in essence different from the more general utopias which have exercised political thinkers. But, as guidelines have to be given more often, as each particular conflict may in practice be considered separately without reference to a general philosophy of society, discussions on guidelines remain at times divorced from the more comprehensive thinking of the utopia-builders. The complexity of utopias, their apparent lack of realism, the difficulties which they raise when it comes to moving from grand principles to concrete conflicts of goals, all lead to many discussions on guidelines for action independent of utopia-building. Whatever may be thought about ideal freedom or ideal democracy, the choice of the details of an electoral law, for example, may often be related to the need to find a practical compromise between fair campaigning – which means equality for all the candidates – and the freedom to propagate ideas – which means that the richer candidates have a greater scope; similarly, a balance has to be struck between the need for frequent popular elections and the value of giving to those elected a sufficient breathing space to implement policies.

Applied normative thinking is thus a very common endeavour of those who think politically. First, it is often associated with technical prescription: normative guidelines can only be given once the empirical problems have been examined. As empirical problems are usually complex and difficult to analyse systematically, technical prescription and the choice of guidelines are often intertwined, to the detriment of both normative thinking and descriptive analysis. The result is that neither are empirical points established, nor guidelines provided. If it is not known what type of party system leads to executive stability in a parliamentary context, it is not possible to give the normative reasons for preferring a strong executive to a more divided, but perhaps more representative, party system. Second, in comparison with other sciences, political thinking discovers very few scientific laws; guidelines are therefore often reduced to temporary expedients. While what is needed is a true combination of descriptive study and normative analysis, the result is often a difficult and unchallenging compromise where neither type of approach is able to show its rigour.

The tension between normative and descriptive political science is here to stay: mankind will always search for goals, yet no descriptive analysis can define these goals empirically and make the appropriate choices. Moralism, as legalism or historicism, does make exaggerated claims in political analysis. But those who wish to develop a more scientific discipline will not gain by attempting to dislodge normative political thought. The conflict may often be acute: it reflects two profoundly different intellectual standpoints. Any reductionist outlook impoverishes the discipline, makes it less able to answer the questions for which it came to exist and leads to further tensions.

Those who think politically thus span a range of approaches which are almost as wide as the whole catalogue of human intellectual endeavours. Whether the 'scientists' wish to destroy it or not, the 'artistic' side of political thinking is an important component of the discipline. It suggests ideas about a future society; it gives an impression of the lives of great men and of the overall climate which accompanies great events. It has its limits, admittedly: not all utopias are poetic in style and presentation and care has to be a characteristic of historical analyses, whether of great men and events or of regular happenings. Meanwhile, on the more scientific side, logic, but also mathematics, as well as the painstaking collecting of evidence, suggest comparisons with economics and physics (or even with chemistry and biology) due to the number of elements and variables which political thinkers have to examine and assess, control or pigeonhole for even the simplest of their analyses.

Political thinking needs more than the mere juxtaposition of these approaches if it is to achieve its aims. Yet the tension at times is such that little communication or cross-fertilization occurs between the supporters of the various points of view. For real unity to exist there must be, behind differences of approach, some common concern and a common method. It is, of course, unrealistic to expect all those who think politically to have, to the same extent, this concern and this method. But only if common elements are present in at least much of political thinking and at crucial crossroads can it be more than a kaleidoscopic collection of separate viewpoints and truly deserve the name of discipline.

CHAPTER 3

The common concern of those who think politically

Now that we have at least an impression of the many approaches in political science, we can see whether some unity emerges from this variety; whether the differences within the discipline constitute more discord than in other disciplines. From the outside, at least, controversies between political scientists do not seem markedly greater than between those who study physics, biology, or the other social sciences.[1] If there is to be unity between those who study politics, the various approaches must represent different outlooks of a common concern. So we must first try and see whether, perhaps unconsciously, the supporters of a particular approach find themselves obliged to adopt lines or standpoints reminiscent of other approaches. And we must, more importantly, ascertain whether the differences in approach are an intrinsic part of such a many-faceted science as politics.

I.   *The 'negative' links between those who think politically: some insidious relationships between the various approaches*
    A. *The common phenomenon of the normative-cum-descriptive approach.* We stressed in the previous chapter the profound

---

[1] The history of physics and astronomy has been that of major disagreement from the Middle Ages to the present day: the attacks against Galileo, for instance, were not just against the substance of his findings, but against the methods used, since these were held to be invalid. The disputes between 'Lamarckians' and 'Darwinians' in biology lasted for a large part of the nineteenth century. In economics, Keynesian ideas only became widely adopted after considerable opposition and, indeed, mainly because traditional economic theory could not handle the problems of the Great Depression.

differences between a descriptive (or at times technically prescriptive) approach and one which concentrates on analysing
basic goals. Yet few studies concentrate exclusively on either
norms or description without implying the need for a combination of both. Some factual analyses concentrate on the meticul-
ous description of a particular question; but this will be related,
either overtly or covertly, to broader perspectives.

Descriptive works sometimes claim to contribute to building
up a bank of knowledge which would enable the laws of politics
to be discovered. As we noted in the previous chapter, the search
for such laws goes back at least as far as Aristotle, though Montesquieu was perhaps the first to give it systematic expression.[2]
Hope and disillusionment succeeded each other regularly.
Modern behaviourism has had some successes: for instance,
many relationships between socio-economic development and
liberal democracy have been found, including correlations between kinds of regimes (for instance military regimes) and
phases of economic development.[3] Yet though studies of this
kind aim at producing general laws in a descriptive or technically prescriptive fashion, they also incorporate a normative
element. It has even been suggested by some, mainly critics with
radical views, that a scientific approach is indeed a misnomer,
because the selection of topics, the definition of the concepts, the
choice of the indicators, imply assumptions of a normative character reflecting the values of those engaged in the research. The
assumptions may often be concealed: it may be assumed, for
instance, that stability is a 'good thing' in itself; one then finds
that stability can only be achieved, in a liberal democracy, if
there is an element of apathy, since too much involvement on
the part of too many will lead to conflict and the survival of the
system may be endangered.[4] In such a case, because the goal is

[2] Montesquieu begins the *Spirit of Laws* (1748) by the following paragraph:
'Laws in their broadest sense are the necessary relations which are derived
from the nature of things and, in this sense, all beings have their laws: God has
his laws; the physical world has its laws; beings more intelligent than men
have their laws; beasts have their laws; man has his laws.'
[3] Among the many studies on this problem, see in particular R. A. Dahl,
Polyarchy (Yale University Press, New Haven, 1971).
[4] See, particularly in connection with apathy, the attack against 'behavioural
standpoints' in W. Berns's 'Voting Studies' in H. J. Storing, ed., *Essays on the
scientific study of politics* (Holt, Rinehart & Winston, New York, 1952).

not made explicit, any normative element is subsumed under conditional prescription.

The more extreme of these critics of descriptive techniques claim that all analysis implies a defence or attack of certain systems, merely by choosing them as topics of discussion. The extension of the argument is that, rather than pretend objectivity, one should admit to applying norms at the outset of research.

While there is some validity in this criticism, the converse is, of course, also true: namely, that purely normative analyses are rare and indeed impossible. Those who claim to be defending a value judgment do so by a mixture of normative assertions and empirical statements, many of which remain unproven and are usually advanced too quickly as being 'self-evident'. It was precisely because these statements were unproven that behavioural political scientists endeavoured to build a more scientific approach. 'Classical' political writers are often presented as normative; yet from Aristotle to the present day, all political theorists have made empirical statements; even utopian thinkers related their analyses largely to the real world.[5]

To be wholly normative would imply making only statements of preference, without reference to reality or possibilities of implementation. In fact people usually want to know what are the chances of success of their chosen systems. If a utopia is to be a goal for future generations, it must in some way relate to man's experience. There is an underlying belief in the role of ideas in bringing about changes which implies an *empirical* theory, though the assumption is rarely openly stated and even more rarely discussed. There are also suggested developments and suggested chains of events: these are *descriptive* statements linking the existing society to the ideal society which is being

[5] The following statements, chosen at random from among the 'classics', give an impression of the type of descriptive statement that can be repeatedly found in these works – statements which are rarely, if at all, backed by 'scientific evidence'.
Hobbes: 'Nature has made men so equal in the faculties of body and mind . . . When all is reckoned together, the difference between man and man is not so considerable as that one man can thereupon claim to himself any benefit to which another may not pretend as well as he.' (*Leviathan*, book 1, chapter 13).
Aristotle: 'Nature has distinguished between female and slave.' (*Politics*, book 1, chapter 2).

proposed. Indeed even the pure utopian who claims to write about a society which will never take place is an empiricist: it is an empirical point to suggest that the proposed utopian blueprint will never be implemented! Hobbes wanted to give a blueprint for the absolutist State: he based his proposal on man's life being 'nasty, brutish and short'; which was an empirical, not a normative assumption. When Rousseau stated that 'man is in chains' and built on this claim much of his call for change in society, he made an empirical statement, though he did not really prove it scientifically.

Some claim that every *statement* is normative-cum-descriptive; but one could only maintain this view by including in this category the very statement that claims this point to be true. It would not be very helpful in real-world analysis and it is therefore best left to philosophers for consideration. But there is clearly a close link between normative and descriptive approaches in political thinking. The normative approach needs to be supported by descriptions to have a grip on reality and thus to convince its readers, while a purely descriptive analysis that does not relate, at least indirectly, to the ethical problem of man in society remains unimportant. Analyses of leadership in government, of the electoral process and electoral behaviour, of legislatures, parties and interest groups, of the military, of great men, all involve the relationship between people and government – a question which in turn leads to problems of liberty and of democracy.

B. *Legalism and realism.* The association between legalism and realism is similar to that between normative and descriptive approaches. In a number of ways, the work of political scientists is a constant mixture of the examination of structures and the study of behaviour. Norms and structures are also related, as we

---

Rousseau: 'Man is born free and everywhere is in chains.' (*Social Contract*, book 1, chapter 1).

Paine: 'Government is no farther necessary than to supply the few cases to which society and civilisation are not conveniently competent; and instances are not wanting to show that everything which government can usefully add thereto has been performed by the common consent of society, without government.' (*Rights of Man*, part 2, chapter 1).

Mill: 'Having said that the individuality is the same thing with development and that it is only the cultivation of individuality which produced or can produce well-developed human beings . . .' (*On Liberty*, chapter 3).

saw previously. Since new structures are introduced to implement new norms – an empirical point which is not proven but
which everyone accepts in practice – it is further assumed that
behaviour will be changed: otherwise, why should a *structure* be
introduced? Those who look at behaviour cannot avoid taking
into account existing structures, nor can students of structures,
procedures or laws be wholly unconcerned by the behavioural
effects: otherwise why should they suggest *new* laws? Thus
norms, structures and behaviour are indissolubly linked.

Pure studies of behaviour are therefore necessarily narrow:
they have an impact only within the framework of structures.
This is one of the main reasons why electoral studies have been
unsuccessful at explaining patterns of voting behaviour on a
world-wide basis. Despite considerable efforts in the last few
decades, many studies, a very large infra-structure and much
expenditure, voting behaviour studies have remained constrained by the electoral system and the party system of the
country studied. They are therefore never truly general – even in
countries where the electoral context is competitive they remain
relevant only in a specific context.[6] The same goes for studies of
the behaviour of committees, legislatures and governments. All
behaviourists have to become involved in studying structures or
risk seeing their work narrowly circumscribed.

C. *Hopes for generalizations but many examples.* The same
difficulty affects the controversy between generalizations and
detailed analyses. We have seen that many political scientists
often seek variables and indicators, only to find the results un-
reliable or at best falling far short of their ideal; the goal of
expressing relationships linking phenomena in truly scientific

[6] Voting studies became increasingly sophisticated in the course of the 1950s
and 1960s and have drawn to a considerable extent on the techniques of
statistics and mathematics. Yet their framework is primarily country-bound:
the tendency for electors to vote for one party rather than for another has to
take into account the strength of the parties, their number, as well as the
electoral system. Thus one finds American, British, French, Swedish or Ger-
man studies of elections, but it is difficult to go beyond a country. The nearest
example – which is not a voting study proper, but a study of the underlying
bases of voting behaviour – to a cross-national study is that of R. R. Alford,
Party and Society (Rand McNally, Chicago, 1963); yet this study is concerned
only with the four major 'Anglo-American' democracies, America, Canada,
Australia and Britain.

terms remains a distant dream. It is difficult to express structures in terms of variables, as structures are so complex that they cannot easily be analysed, weighed and compared.

Generalizations have therefore often been pious hopes or have been imprisoned in the somewhat dubious mould of the 'typical case'. And even typical cases constitute uneasy compromises between generalizations and supporting factual evidence: generalizations are usually buttressed by a whole series of examples, which, in spite of their numbers, often meet only part of the requirements, even as illustrations, let alone in logic. In the case of the study of comparative government in particular, which is torn between models and streams of examples, whenever an author attempts generalizations, the facts he draws on are examples from only *some* countries, at only *some* point, and only in a *given* context.[7]

Hence the difficulty of generalization. It is not that authors do not wish to generalize; it is not that they do not believe in the generalization ideal as an ultimate goal for the discipline. But structures, events and situations need to be described. Examples are chosen because the scope for generalizations is very limited: they show the honesty of those who are involved in the difficult process of giving a framework to the whole discipline. Even the most convinced generalizer cannot fail to respond to the uniqueness of individual events. Unconsciously perhaps, generalizers are drawn 'down' to the facts, often so much so that the jumps between 'grand models' and detailed examples are difficult to follow; this leads to suggestions that more work should be done at the 'middle-range' level.[8] Historical viewpoints rarely disappear in the honest exposition of general ideals.

But it does not follow that unique events are the only basis for

[7] A good example of this process can be found in G. A. Almond and G. B. Powell, *Comparative Politics* (Little, Brown, Boston, 1966), *passim,* where the authors have a general model of the process of government cross-nationally, and yet base their generalizations on a number of examples only. This is particularly true of Chapters 9 and 10, which examine the various 'types' of political systems.

[8] For an argument in favour of this viewpoint, see J. LaPalombara, 'Macro-theories and microapplications in Comparative politics' in *Comparative politics,* 1 (1968), pp. 52-78.

the analysis as much of the detailed work leads to general assertions and interpretations. In studying the history of great men
and events or the idiosyncratic characteristics of structures and
systems, generalizations often come to be made. A case will be
studied, for instance, the 'making' of a president or of a prime
minister, because it is claimed to be typical and thereby helps to
relate to other practices or tends to illuminate a whole institution. A leader will be studied because he will have either displayed the characteristics of some types of leaders or because his
'influence' on his country (a generalization) or the political
system (another generalization) is felt to be large (and hopefully
shown to be so). This means that 'influence' is viewed as an
important general concept. Rarely is a revolution studied for its
own sake: causes (which are generalizations) and consequences
(from which general lessons are drawn) help to give the event a
further dimension which goes beyond the bounds of narrative
history. Moreover, assumptions about human nature – for
instance relating to a particular culture – are rarely absent from
studies of events. They may be made cautiously and thus help to
limit hasty generalizations which could easily characterize –
and sometimes do characterize – the examination of more than
one culture and more than one period. But they rarely propose
to leave completely aside the possible lessons of such an enterprise and thus contribute in part to the generalization process
which they claim to prevent.

Both the unique and the general are profoundly embedded in
the tradition of thinking politically as twin elements which can
never for long be wholly dissociated. In this, as we saw, structures play a large part. It is the presence of structures which
prevents wider generalizations, because structures emphasize
difference between countries and between groups. A Conservative Party in Britain differs culturally from a Conservative Party
in Sweden or Denmark; the United States Congress differs culturally from the British Parliament. Yet, paradoxically, structures are also the basis for generalizations, as they are lasting
umbrellas, which give unity to large groups of facts – since they
last over time – and thus force those who are inclined to examine
special cases to consider at least similarities over a period and
between countries as well.

The study of comparative government has been particularly

affected by this difficulty, because of the role that facts (events, statesmen) and structures (parties, legislatures) have always played in the life of governments. No student of government clings so strongly to the unique that he refuses to look at the role of structures, such as political parties; typical textbook questions demand comparisons between government and parliament, between the American President and the British Prime Minister, all of which require the examination over time or space of many cases in order to find patterns and draw contrasts. No extreme generalizer could succeed in abandoning for long the narration of facts. Models may be beautiful: but they can only be helpful if, in the last resort, they do help to illuminate facts.

Political thinkers are constantly torn between the many lines of approach which characterize their discipline. Every political scientist, or almost every one, has internalized these approaches. There may be times when one approach, or some approaches, appear to dominate: some are *more* inclined towards one approach, or may even be the prisoners of the postures which they took. But the pendulum of opinion gradually swings back in the other direction. Few are the political thinkers who do not either recognize the need for compromise or are not forced in practice to use other approaches in order to prove their points: partly because of the difficulty and diffuseness of the discipline and the inability to discover methods which are wholly adequate; partly because, as we saw, the problems raised are ambiguous, straddle both values and techniques and are never, or at least rarely, only in one camp. There are therefore links between the approaches: this surely does denote some fairly common view about the subject-matter and some instinctive agreement about the broad problems that will need to be solved as the discipline improves.

II.   *Political scientists and politics*
   A. *The idea of politics: what politics is for those who think politically.*
In the absence of any evidence, it is of course impossible to state categorically that all those who think politically agree on a common definition of politics and view in the same way at least the problems which they have to solve, if not their solutions. But the works of political scientists do not suggest profound

disagreements on what characterizes a political problem.

Admittedly, over time, definitions of politics have tended to change and the scope of political activity has been conceived of in a broader fashion. For a period during the nineteenth century, due to the influence of lawyers on political science, particularly in Europe, political activity was conceived of in terms of the State, viewed as a legal entity. This is no longer accepted: nor was it accepted at the time of the Greeks or during the Middle Ages, since the notion of the State is a product of the Renaissance and can be viewed as the result of the efforts of monarchs to increase administrative centralization to their benefit. In fact, there were no rigid definitions either during the period of the emergence of the State or during much of the subsequent period: politics was accepted as being primarily concerned with the activities of the *polis* (the city), and secondarily concerned with the *politeia* (the State).[9] These two expressions originally had precise connotations, particularly the first, since it was a description of the 'City-State'. But they came increasingly to be viewed as abstractions referring to a form of 'common' activity and even the geographical base ceased to be an unreal prerequisite. The prevailing trend, indeed the overwhelmingly accepted view, suggests that politics relates to activities taking place in an abstract *polis,* that is a common body, often geographical, but more because this is so in practice than as a matter of principle.

Thus, first, politics relates to activities taking place in common, activities taking place in a society. The individual enters politics insofar as he has an impact on or is subjected to a common activity. But this definition will not suffice, since all social activities *do* take place in common. Politics occurs, not just *because* a society exists where the activity occurs, as for instance the market's existence would constitute the stage for (some) economics. The activity *itself* must be common. Politics relates to *common decisions,* that is decisions which are applicable to all

[9] See R. M. Maciver, *The modern state* (Oxford, 1926), Book I. 'The emergence of the State' for an examination of the development of the idea of the State, from the Greek City-State to the Roman and Byzantine Empires and later to the modern notion of the State. Aristotle in his *Politics* can be considered as the founder of the study of political science in the descriptive sense, but his view of the 'State' is limited to the *polis.*

those who do belong to this community. At first unconsciously, gradually increasingly consciously, those who thought about politics felt they were concerned with decisions, and in particular, those decisions that affected the whole community.

Of course, historically, political thinkers did not come directly to this definition. What was first apparent was that profound cleavages opposed individuals and groups and that 'something had to be done' to prevent these oppositions from degenerating. Thinkers of this type (such as Hobbes, and possibly also Aristotle) were primarily concerned with maintaining peace in the *polis*. Others, like Marx or Rousseau, were more concerned with the injustices that they saw around them, such as the existence of a class of poor and very poor. They felt that existing conditions perpetuated these injustices and believed that major changes were necessary to achieve greater equality. But whether or not they suggested consciously that the study of politics was *about* these large conflicts, they were concerned with problems for which a decision had to be found for the whole community. With time, political thinkers have come gradually to refine the definition by becoming clearer about their object of study; they now recognize that they inquire into problems which have to be solved at the community level by making decisions which are applicable to the whole community; political scientists are thus broadly concerned with the analysis of collective goods.[10]

The exact definition of 'collective goods' is an object of controversy, admittedly. Some claim that almost anything is a collective good. A decision that individuals in a community have the right to choose when to spend their 'own' money, for example, must affect others in the community, either because prices of certain products will vary according to individual whims rather than according to community decisions, or because the community will be involved in using resources (labour, capital) in the production of these goods in proportions

[10] The notion of 'collective good' has become prevalent in modern political science, particularly in works which attempt to apply some economic techniques to politics, but in a transformed fashion. See, for example, M. Olson Jr., *The Logic of Collective Action* (Harvard University Press, Cambridge, Mass., 1965). One should note, however, that this view was in fact implied from the very start in large numbers of studies, from Aristotle to the present day: much of Mill's *Liberty* is in fact concerned with problems of this type.

which might be different were the whole community to decide on them. One can thus discover what might be called a 'maximalist' and a 'minimalist' view of politics, with an infinity of positions between these two extremes: the maximalist position views as *potentially* collective any good (or service) that exists in the community or may be produced by the community, unless it is not rare (and, with the pollution of air, it becomes difficult to be sure that there is any good that is not in fact rare); the Left adopts this viewpoint. The minimalist position, on the contrary, sees politics as being restricted to those matters which cannot be decided at all *except* on the basis of a common approach: for instance, the decision of whether to go to war or not, which must be taken for the whole community, or the question of whether to drive on the left or the right of the road.

In the last hundred years maximalism has gained ground in the world at large, but one must not forget that earlier periods were marked by very heavy doses of maximalism. The industrial and commercial revolutions of the early nineteenth century, on the other hand, can be seen as victories for minimalism over the previous ideas of maximalism.

Yet, whatever differences there may be about the definition of 'collective good', political thinkers agree that, once a good is viewed as collective, it becomes subject to decisions of a political kind. One can therefore see why the notion of conflict is both quite critical, and yet only a corollary to the definition of politics. Politics is not about conflict as such. But, quite naturally, political thinkers became primarily concerned with those problems which either were already or were potentially sources of conflict in communities. The more acute the conflict (real or imagined), the more they were concerned with the problem, since these political thinkers were likely to be emotionally pressed to find a solution. Political activity is not caused by conflict, it is caused by the disagreements over collective goods and the need to allocate them. The conflict is likely to be large for most collective goods; and, in view of the division between maximalism and minimalism, the area of collective goods will vary and conflict will emerge when a problem comes to be perceived as a collective good. Some political thinkers (Aristotle and Hobbes, for instance) seem to have been mainly interested in peace and a decrease in civil strife; but Aristotle recognized

that very important collective goods were at stake behind questions of civil strife – and his aim was to solve these problems in
order to bring about peace. Even Hobbes, who thought that
strife was an inevitable product of human nature, rated peace
(our modern idea of law and order) the most important of all
collective goods.

An important and general question lies behind this problem,
that of authority. Some modern political scientists, such as
Easton, have defined politics as the 'authoritative allocation of
values'.[11] However, since a common decision made about
values, goods or services is applicable to everyone, at least in
theory, it is strictly unnecessary to add that the allocation
should be 'authoritative'. In fact the very word 'allocation' implies authority. But the point is important, as it suggests that the
mechanics of decision-making and the means through which decisions are enforced are crucial elements of political life. We
need not examine here the various types of obedience, but
simply note the point that *some* form of obedience has to exist in
any society as, otherwise, no collective good would ever be implemented. Whether decisions are taken by all or a few, one
critical question, perhaps the most critical of all, is that of consent. This is why some political thinkers, such as Hobbes, were
concerned almost exclusively with questions of peace and war or
law and order. Naturally enough, in times of strife or civil war, a
major and prior objective is to restore authority, since when
there is no authority (no authority at all) no decision is taken. If
the breakdown of authority takes geographical lines, as with
secession, there may be an authority within each of the parts.
But where there is no authority, where there is true 'lawlessness',
there is no means of taking decisions on any collective good.
Politics disappears because there can be no allocation of any
value.

B. *The intractable questions.* From this impression of what politics is about, a number of problems emerge: the awareness of
these problems contributes as much as the definition of politics
to giving a common concern to those who think politically. One
problem is that ends can never be wholly separated from means:
decisions have to be taken, but how decisions are taken is linked

[11] See D. Easton, *The Political System* (Knopf, New York, 1953), p.126

unavoidably to what they are about. Another problem is due to 'hard' structures breaking the 'flow' of 'happenings': authorities which decide are at least as important as the decisions themselves. Yet another problem is due to the constraints which stem from the chain which links ends to means or ties the behaviour to the pattern of structures.

(i) *Means and ends.* We did not circumscribe the field of collective goods, as 'matters' which require common decisions can be extended or restricted according to the view – maximalist or minimalist – which thinkers hold about the 'proper' scope of collective goods in society. All that can be said is that at any given point in time in a given community, a matter will be 'collective' when a sizeable segment perceives that decisions on this matter should be made collectively. Nothing is intrinsically a collective good; all matters have the potential to be collective goods.

Since everything might be a collective good, would it not be more logical to argue that the main object of political activity is to process decisions, and thus that politics is devoted to means, or, as is often said, to procedures? Like a conveyor belt, the political process turns desires into decisions: if large numbers of people want bread to be distributed free instead of sold, bread ceases to be a merchandise for which economic laws are allowed to prevail and becomes a collective good. If large numbers of people feel that gambling is reprehensible, the question of gambling has to be treated as a collective good: it is no longer left to the choice of each individual. This is where conflict comes to play a part: it is an indication of when a problem needs to be decided as a collective good. As long as there is no conflict about the status quo, there is a tendency to 'forget problems' (or to leave them to be solved outside of politics); when conflict arises, they can no longer be ignored.

Such a view suggests that there is no particular content to the field of politics: if anything can become the subject of political conflict, nothing in particular is by its nature a political matter. Yet such a procedural line cannot seriously be taken to its ultimate conclusion: to limit the domain of politics to processes is to deny it any ends. There are several objections to such a conclusion: we have already seen that political thinking is inextricably concerned with values; more specifically, it just is not the case that procedures are devised without ends in mind: both thinkers and the public instinctively relate procedures to ends.

It is worth exploring this matter in more detail. Let us suppose first that the aim of political action is to take decisions; even if political activity were to concentrate on devising the best procedures for a society, the problem would not be solved. How can the 'best' procedures be defined? It could be the quickest, the simplest; it could be the most democratic, the most liberal. As there are obviously various definitions of 'best', the one to be chosen would be determined by the thinker's own values. He might choose peace rather than liberty; efficiency and speed rather than democracy. So we inevitably return to the normative view.

But this is not the only objection to the procedural view. In reality political thinkers never believe in one and *only one* basis for all procedures. Conflicts between types of procedures lead them to take the substance of the decision into account as a possible basis for choosing the type of procedure. For instance, no individual, politician or political thinker, is prepared to adopt rule by majority *in all circumstances*: it seems right that some private views be allowed, or that the majority should not be allowed to harass constantly the minority. Some problems are held to be so closely connected with basic human values that rule by majority has to be set aside. Hobbes is often thought to have wanted peace to prevail 'at all costs': in fact he introduced 'conditions' for a sovereign, one of which was the responsibility for protecting the lives of his subjects. Indeed Hobbes's whole thesis depends on the hypothesis (or gamble) that an absolute sovereign will better protect the lives of his subjects. So for Hobbes a 'better' society was a peaceful society; and a peaceful society was an absolutist state. It was this belief that led him to propose the surrender of individual rights.

We must conclude then that any attempt to confine political thinking to means must finally accept the role of ends. The same applies to the opposite argument: that of the philosophical political thinker, whose emphasis on norms overlooks the problem of means. Principles need to be applied, and, when they come to be applied, they quickly raise the question of the 'best' means. No one can be *wholly* disengaged from questions of tactics: no one ever suggests that means and procedures are altogether secondary to goals. Even those who claim to support a particular end 'at all costs' will justify their extreme attitude by *special* conditions. Moreover, 'at all costs' itself gets complicated by considerations of the moral costs, which we already saw, and the tactical costs; the latter clearly can only be calculated by an empirical method.

(ii) *Hard structures and continuous change.* The definition of politics also leads to the intractable problem of the simultaneous existence of fixed elements and a continuous flow of change. We noted that lawyers drew attention to the role of structures; we saw that the study of decisions could not wholly overlook the authorities in charge of making decisions. Political thinking is constantly brought up short by some inflexible elements that impede the course of decision-making; structures and behaviour are as interdependent as are means and ends. Take the word 'authority': it typifies the highly ambiguous and dual aspect of all of politics. To hold authority is, or at least so it seems, to be in a position to influence events. Let us simply recognize – without going into an analysis of the nature of authority – that everybody accepts, perhaps for wholly different reasons, that some individuals do hold some authority. Thus we are confronted with a type of influence which is, if not wholly personal, at least 'personalized'. Yet 'the *authorities*' seem to symbolize a wholly different point: these are structures, permanent or at least durable, abstract and divorced from individual holders. And if it is argued that, in reality, the authority that an individual has only stems from the fact that he belongs to the authorities it will still be the case that personal action (fragile and transitory) must be distinguished from the (structural) role of an abstract element, which, compared to the persons, is 'hard' and durable.

When Hobbes wants men to see a sovereign created, he wants a structure to be built: that structure will be in a position to take the daily and current decisions necessary for the community. Hobbes relates the 'flow of decisions' to the 'structural arrangements' that have to be made. So do Rousseau and Marx, and in fact all political thinkers who have built utopias (which are essentially fixed structures). Even anarchists, such as Proudhon, who claim that structures are unnecessary, suggest that some *form* of community is the best means of taking common decisions.[12] The difficulties which anarchism of the extreme type encounters as soon as an organization is created (to end all organizations) and the constant formation and collapse of these organizations, witness the fact that the problem is intractable. The anarchist political thinker is like a lion who wants to break his cage: by breaking the cage he only hurts himself, as the desire to break *all* organizations is among the reasons for his lack of success.

If we move from committed political thinkers or pamphlet-eers anxious to transform the polity to more dispassionate scholars whose overt aims are to explain political life, the dilemma between structures and decisional flow remains intractable: there is no way of solving the problem by avoiding one aspect and stressing the other. Lawyers or legalists who only consider structures recognize that they are not really concerned with politics: they study structures while implying that there is some reality for which the structures are at best a framework. Often this framework is disregarded and it is constantly changing with the surrounding customs and habits. Much is made of the fact that the British constitution is unwritten and thus adaptable to circumstances; but all constitutions are changed in the same way. Was it assumed, when it was founded, that the American Supreme Court would be involved in deciding the validity of congressional acts? If it was assumed, then why did the American Constitution not say so openly, instead of leaving so much scope for controversy? It was not written into the American Constitution that presidents should not be elected for more than two terms, and yet, until F. D. Roosevelt came, the custom was upheld. The view of the American Supreme Court

---

[12] P. J. Proudhon (1809-65) wrote an attack on property and the capitalist system from an anarchistic point of view; he was violently criticized by Marx, who purported to elaborate a much more 'scientific' form of socialism; but Proudhon continued to have a considerable influence within the socialist movement, particularly in France. However 'anarchistic' Proudhon was, he did suggest some organization, though he felt – much like Rousseau – that State power should be abolished and power should be primarily concentrated at the level of local authorities.

[13] These examples suggest among others, the influence of custom and slow development of the U.S. Constitution. In 1803 a decision of the Supreme Court itself established the role of this body as a court of constitutional review; the Senate had been viewed at the time of Washington as a body which would

that segregation was not constitutional was not prompted by constitutional, but by social change.[13] Constitutions, laws and structures change with the times: they are sometimes amended, but they are often, perhaps more often, simply slowly modified. The basic foundations of structures are continuously being eroded – sometimes slowly, sometimes suddenly: old procedures which have been laid down for generations are suddenly dug up and renovated.

Yet political thinkers cannot concern themselves only with these aspects of change and ignore the constitutional context within which change takes place, though they might thereby make political models neater. They have not been helped, as we know, by the serious difficulties of quantification: politics does not offer the same naturally occurring figures as, say, economics. As we have seen, politics is about decisions – a flow of decisions – about collective goods: the task is thus to measure the components of decisions, to assess the degree of opposition to, and support for, the *status quo,* and to examine the outcome in the light of the forces. One of the component forces is the government, another is the political party; yet a third is the organized group, such as a trade union. The assessment of the influence of these bodies is not directly measurable; they form part of the intractable unique elements which we mentioned in the previous chapter. Thus political scientists are left with rather confusing concepts, either indigenous to the discipline, such as 'power', 'influence', 'authority', or imported from elsewhere, mainly from economics, such as 'exchange', 'trade-off', or 'bargaining', which help to describe and categorize, as we shall see in more detail in the next chapter, the 'flow' of the decisions and the content of 'games' and 'battles'; but they are of little use in describing the precise concrete contours and are certainly not the tools which have at least up to now turned the study of flows into a true science.

One cannot therefore say that it would be more helpful to an understanding of politics to study the flow of change rather than

---

collaborate closely with the executive. When the Supreme Court decides that a law of long standing is unconstitutional (as it did in 1954 over 'separate but equal' arrangements in education in the U.S.), it does in fact change the constitution somewhat by adding another type of 'custom' to the interpretation.

structures themselves. Structures have to be studied because they cannot be reduced (except unsatisfactorily in words) to their components. To abandon the study of structures in politics, at a stage when words such as 'power' and 'exchange' are still only vaguely defined, would be like abandoning the study of atoms and molecules in chemistry before the discovery of electrons. Political scientists are too reasonable or too realistic about facts and instruments to abandon structures. They have to remain ambivalent and cannot make choices: the fixed elements and flux are constant components of political thinking.

(iii) *Constraints as part of political thinking.* We have seen the predicament in which political thinkers find themselves; it suggests that the constraints and difficult choices facing the political thinker are perhaps more serious than in other disciplines. It is sometimes suggested that political thinkers are over-realistic and pessimistic. But even the optimism of the utopians has its limits: even an 'optimist' like Rousseau stated that 'man had to be *forced* to be free'; Plato's 'philosopher-Kings' and Rousseau's 'legislator' were invented to help the State or preserve the ideals of the society; Marx's Communist Party has to provide a vanguard leading to better things. No political thinker, as we said, can wholly avoid problems of organizations: no political thinker can be so utopian as to believe that democracy can be fully implemented or that true liberty can be given to all. Sometimes the utopia is presented, as with More's *Utopia* or Cabet's *Icarie,* as a mere dream of a man who wishes in this way to help society in the right direction; sometimes, as with Marx, there is total silence about the characteristics of the new society, while Rousseau's small city, like Plato's world, exists with definite restraints.[14]

The notion of constraint may not be often mentioned by the thinkers themselves. But it is embedded in the discipline: these chains which bind every political thinker, whether he wishes to

---

[14] Plato did produce in the *Republic* a blueprint of government which has sometimes been described as 'totalitarian' in that much of the life of the inhabitants of his 'utopia' was strictly regulated, power belonging primarily to the 'philosopher-Kings'. Rousseau seemed to realize that men might be moving away from the best arrangements he was devising and thus suggested that a legislator might have to be appointed to act as a catalyst and in some way lead the people or prepare the way for the building up of the State (*Social*

present a new blueprint or aims at describing the 'actual' conditions of political life, are the same chains for all. They are intrinsic to the nature of politics, and they, of course, are the challenge. They explain partly why political scientists like to believe that by going back to first principles, by starting *de novo,* rather than pursuing patiently the build-up of the science, they may make *the* discovery that will change the nature of the problem and once and for all establish new bases for the whole discipline. Fortunately, this effort has proved fruitless – fortunately because, at least from an intellectual, perhaps literary angle, political science has thus been able to attract very important minds who have given the world some of their best writings. But this Sisyphus' task is, of course, infuriating to all those who wish to build, slowly and patiently, a scientific discipline. That these chains can be broken seems very unlikely; yet it seems equally unlikely that future political thinkers will be convinced that they cannot be broken, since politics attracts those who have a passionate desire to change society and propose a better life.

III.   *Political scientists and the ranking of political problems. Macro-and micro-analysis*

It would not be realistic to leave our analysis here, and conclude that the common concern of political thinkers is merely their dilemmas. They face a further difficulty, which arises out of the psychology of political thinking. Means and ends oppose each other and thus constrain each other. Yet they are not perceived as being of the same order, as if they were merely two variables which needed to be 'optimized': ends are usually viewed as 'more important' than means, though in what way is not entirely clear. Means are not less important in that they have to be taken into account less than ends: they are in practice considered both because many believe them to be the real province of

---

Contract, book 2, chapter 7): but his legislator is a catalyst, who prepares the ground, not a legislator in the modern sense.

Thomas More (1480-1535) with his *Utopia* (1516) and E. Cabet (1788-1856) with his *Voyage en Icarie* (1842) are perhaps the best two examples of writers who produce a blueprint which is almost wholly divorced from reality – but with a view to teaching others about what society might be; indeed some communities were founded in America on the model of Cabet's *Icarie,* but with very little success.

political thinking and because they affect the feasibility of the ends; ends do not justify means – means must be evaluated separately. But the importance placed on ends probably reflects a feeling that ends should be established first, and means considered secondarily. The importance of means appears to be a concession to realism.

The same point might be made about the opposition between fixed and continuous, though the dilemma is less emotionally loaded. Anarchists, behaviourists and true scientists, who hope to build a more aesthetically satisfying discipline, might all prefer to look at continuous elements and only accept structures in that they correspond to the real world around them and not to their ideal. Means and ends, continuous flows and hard elements constitute the origins of the constraints on political thinking.

Yet – unlike in economics – the idea of constraint has had little appeal in political science. Few political scientists think of their subject as being a number of constraints which they would put on an equal footing: they seek an optimal solution, and rank the problems according to an ideal. In fact, the various approaches to politics correspond to this rank-ordering. It follows that the normative political thinker views a factual approach as somewhat less important; a behaviourist may consider the concern with norms as the pursuit of a chimera, and so on. The other approaches are at best conceded and perhaps in many cases are deprecated.

A. *The distinction between macro- and micro-analysis in political thinking.* This ranking does not exist only in the imagination of political scientists: it is deeply engrained in the minds of many, if not all interested observers of political life. In order to understand the point better, let us leave the general problem for a moment and concentrate on one of its aspects which, though perhaps not sufficiently emphasized, does play a major part in establishing rankings. In the opening paragraph of this book, we noted a contradiction: in various circles 'politics' is a dirty word; yet *no one* considers that it is a dirty game to try to avoid a war or to try to pass a law designed to limit or prevent racial prejudice in housing or transport. Opponents of these moves may suggest that the proponents of peace or racial integration are also trying to advance their own advantage by supporting these measures, but they do not suggest that the measures themselves, *per se,* are intrinsically shabby or of little import.

The point here is not to examine the personal reasons which may lead people to blame 'politicians' in general while being ready to recognize that much of politics is of effective and positive value. It may be that the dislike for individual politicians is such that the term 'politics' becomes associated with the moves of these politicians. What is more important, however, is to assess whether there are indeed any real substantive differences between various aspects of politics which might also account for a broad distinction. Does a division which places 'politics' in one category while assigning to 'statesmanship', for instance, matters such as peace-keeping or racial integration correspond to some real distinction in the nature of the political process?

Differences in vocabulary help to approach this problem. In English, two different words are applied to the two usages – 'politics' and 'policy'; in some other languages, only one word (in French *politique*) corresponds to both meanings. 'Politics' and, by association, 'politician' have 'bad' connotations; 'policy', on the other hand, seems to refer to more exalted issues. There may be 'wrong' and even 'shabby' policies; but many policies are good, useful, even grand. Indeed, if the policy is worthwhile, those who propound it cease to be 'politicians' and become 'statesmen'.

Of course, *all* politicians are involved in policies: but many other activities accompany the policy-making process. Policies are the *substantive* activities of politicians, to be sure; they are what politicians produce, in the same way as a car factory has as its *substantive* role that of producing cars. But not all employees do in fact produce cars: many manage other workers, pay wages and salaries, hire builders to provide new offices and plants, or cook meals. In a similar way, many subsidiary activities are part of the process of policy-making. These subsidiary activities are often held to be useless or at best neutral; they lead to criticisms and are often branded as being responsible for the high costs of products. Thus one should perhaps not be surprised if the subsidiary activities of politicians are not held in good repute by the cynical public.

What activities of politicians constitute these subsidiary functions? Their range is vast, and so is their number. They

consist in campaigning for elections, holding meetings with
diplomats and other representatives of the foreign nations,
selecting committee chairmen or dismissing ministers. They
seem to have one common characteristic, and one which leads to
many criticisms from the outside public. They seem to revolve
around the process of personality building and unbuilding, the
selection of candidates, the blocking of positions. They belong
precisely to the group of activities that the public – and politicians and political scientists as well – condemn as 'political
games'. While policy-making is typically viewed as an activity
lasting over a period and involving planning, rationality and
imagination, the 'jockeying for positions' is seen as a mere game
where selfishness is the motive and which indeed distracts the
attention of politicians and public from the true aim of public
life which should be to concentrate on policies.

Two points should be noted. First, there is clearly a relationship between internal politics – the politics of positions – and
external or output politics. Clearly the latter have to be initiated
by someone and therefore there will be competition for positions
of responsibility. Internal or personal politics need the politics of
outputs to exist at all. Policies proposed and policies previously
decided help politicians to be better or less well placed in the
games which they play. It may be thought at first that personal
battles are of little value to the community; but there are many
ways in which these personal fights can help, at least when they
do not assume major proportions. We may claim that we would
like conflicts to concentrate on standpoints and programmes; in
fact we often personalize these conflicts and understand them
better as a result. These games can also help to show which
politicians are best suited to administer or manage specific
policies. So it is an oversimplification and a mistake to dismiss
the personal part of politics as mere political 'games'.

The second point is the converse: while there is a link between
external and internal politics, there is also a marked cleavage,
which may in some circumstances lead to a complete isolation of
each of the spheres. In some cases it might even be true to say
that both parts of politics operate on different planes, and
therefore obey different rules, with great consequences for political life and for political thinking.

There are three major differences between the two aspects of politics. First, 'internal' politics is normally face-to-face while 'external' politics is mostly between 'strangers'; second, internal politics is continuous, while external politics takes place occasionally, in the form of separate statements on separate policies; and third, internal politics is concerned with personal careers (even if the men involved are part-timers or are unpaid), while external politics concerns almost all citizens, most of whom have no professional or career stake in what is going on. Only in small committees (parishes, tiny associations) do the two aspects become combined; in larger communities, whether nations or local authorities, the distinction is very marked indeed. Only in small units are the leaders chosen among friends and continue to live among these friends. In political groups of any significance, the two aspects are dissociated: leaders are separated from the led both geographically and in their psychological involvement in the political process.

This is why it is true to say that there are indeed two *forms* of politics, related to be sure, and even merging in the exceptional case of small groups, but typically quite distinct. Internal politics should properly be designated 'micro-politics' – 'micro' because it is composed of small groups of individuals – while external politics is 'macro-politics', as it related to the whole polity. One can therefore assume that there will be profound differences between patterns of behaviour in both types of politics and, at the extremes, that one might be dealing with two distinct worlds. A suitable analogy might be the distinction between the two movements of the earth: its rotation on its own axis and its rotation round the sun. Though the two movements are interconnected, different rules are applicable to each.

Some rules do tend to apply to one type of politics more than to the other. For instance 'trade-off' plays a very large part in 'micro-politics', while it is of little consequence in 'macro-politics'. More generally, time plays a different part in the two environments. In micro-politics, changes are rapid and easy to follow; in macro-politics, movements are usually slow and, partly as a result, difficult to observe. We might perhaps use again the analogy with the movements of the earth. Ephemeral creatures are not affected by the seasonal movements of the earth, only of the daily movement producing day and night. Politicians are quite ephemeral: most of them have only a few

years of really active service, particularly if one excludes years of
'apprenticeship' from 'productive' life. For them – at least for
many – micro-politics is the real politics. They find it difficult to
perceive that one could or should be bothered with some very
general views or with long-term changes in the political process;
if a policy just cannot be adopted in a given situation, they often
regard efforts to overcome the whole situation and introduce
ideal arrangements as a waste of time; if any political thinker
should suggest doing so, he is therefore often considered as providing proof that political thinkers are hopelessly impractical.
Of course not all politicians live this ephemeral life; some are
truly concerned with going beyond political games, others are
secure in their position and a few simply do not care if their
tenure of office is very short indeed. But few politicians are not at
least somewhat schizophrenic about the whole issue, as 'internal' politics, or 'politics as a game', is a vital part of their activity,
an activity which they must at least enjoy minimally if they are
to live with it.

The opposite is true for the public, even the political public:
for them internal politics is both a mystery and a great illusion.
They may be interested at times in purely personal games in the
few cases when micro-politics escalates on to the public forum.
The abdication of a king, the selection of a new prime minister
by a small caucus or of a presidential candidate by a larger con-
vention, or battles between ministers may occasionally lead the
public to take an interest. But they are soon seen to be games
which do not affect the life of the common man. Cynicism often
creeps in – as was the case before 1958 with the selection of
French Prime Ministers, which was held to be a joke by most
French citizens.

Political scientists are caught in the middle: they know that
micro-politics does exist, and has to exist; but many of them, like
many ordinary citizens, find micro-politics sordid. To explain
that much of politics falls inevitably into the micro category,
due to the very nature of the political process, is clearly one of
the important duties of political scientists. Yet observers of
politics will none the less often react against this inevitable
aspect of political life and may indeed switch to apathy or even
open revolt.

Perhaps the most important aspect of the distinction between micro- and macro-politics is not the difference in rules or the variations in the duration of each cycle. It is that micro-politics is primarily behavioural, while macro-politics takes place almost entirely through the links created by structures in the political system. In micro-politics, the politician is the actor: he jockeys for positions, makes deals with othes, recompenses others for favours. In macro-politics, the actor is, to a very large extent, the institution or the procedure.

Of course, structures – whether institutions or procedures – play some part in micro-politics; but they are only a framework. Micro-politics is affected by the conditions created by the structures: the parliamentary system relates ministers to backbenchers in a different fashion from the presidential system, for instance; executive decision-making is equally affected by the framework of the organization of the Cabinet, where decisions may or may not be taken collectively and according to a whole variety of procedures. In macro-politics, however, structures are not merely the framework: the whole process takes place through and in the structures. Face-to-face relations – discussions, bargaining, personal influence – are replaced by the more anonymous relations between the structures – speeches to large audiences, written petitions or orders, elections, etc. Political reactions take place through a structure. In a face-to-face situation, voting is the result of discussion; it takes place on a whole variety of small and big issues; in macro-politics, voting is only exceptionally on a single decision, and, if so, as with referendums, it is always about a broad problem; generally, voting at the macro level relates to parties or to men and women who represent a party or a broad political spectrum. Thus the structure – the party, for instance – is the medium through which the communication between leaders and led takes place. More generally, interest groups of all kinds form the basic elements in the chain which links the public with political leaders; bureaucracies, courts, the military are all further elements connecting people and politics. Even leaders of the charismatic type have to create structures if they wish to maintain their position and 'perpetuate' their influence. Thus political thinking entails constantly moving from a plane in which individual actions play a considerable part to one where the structures and their development are the main elements of political life.

B. *Political thinking and the relationship between norms, structures and behaviour.* We can now return to the general problem of 'gradations' in political thinking. In our survey of political thinking we identified three types of abstractions which form the elements of the analysis. These are *values* or norms (the technical distinction between the two concepts is that norms are more specific than values),[15] *structures* (which include institutions and procedures) and *behaviour* or happenings (which constitute the 'facts' of political life). Though the three elements are related, political thinkers differ in the priorities they allot to each.

Because of the ostensible importance of ends, norms and values are often seen as the apex of the pyramid of political thinking. We know that ends inescapably involve means; and that means draw one on to a consideration of implementation: which in turn leads to a consideration of structures and behaviour. Yet political thinkers are often persuaded that their analyses should be purely conducted on the level of norms.

Normative theory has thus constructed a variety of models, such as the Marxist model: these 'package deals' can be accepted or rejected *en bloc* by politicians and public. The development of models has been the contribution of political thinkers for generations. The quantity is vast, and it is not possible, in the course of this short book, to give even a limited idea of the richness and variety of all these package deals: nor is it, perhaps, necessary. But we shall have at least to consider further the extent to which these models have affected others in the history of political thought.

Normative theory can be pursued autonomously, at least in so far as it is the apex of political inquiry; but its impact on structures and behaviour, though inevitable, remains much of a mystery. Because a significant part of the study of structures relates to change in the *status quo* or to the maintenance of the *status quo* against opposition, the problem of structures is closely tied to the study of norms. While some normative theorists may reject structures on principle, and prefer behavioural approaches directly proceeding from the study of means, we

[15] On the distinction between values and norms in the technical sense, see N. Smelser, *A Theory of Collective Behaviour* (Routledge & Kegan Paul, London, 1962), pp. 24 ff.

have seen how this cannot but fail. A link does exist: structures are created or maintained in order to affect behaviour in the future. But the link is obscure and only in special circumstances can a precise relationship be shown to exist: it seems none the less to follow that structures should be ranked below values; they appear to proceed from norms and owe their content to them.

But norms only explain structures in part: there is also an interplay between the structures. Jointly, institutions and procedures form *systems*; the institutions of the parliamentary form of government or of the Soviet one-party State are examples of such systems. This is why political thinking has to be concerned with the interrelations between structures. This, too, leads to theory. Such an institutional or structural theory may still be inchoate; it may not as yet satisfactorily explain the internal mechanics of build-up or decay of structures; only occasionally is it able to establish rules of compatibility or of consistency. But it is striving towards this goal, which is no less important than the goal of normative theory. Indeed, in some of its aspects, particularly in relation to legal arrangements, institutional theory has led to general practical applications. As well as examining the ways in which political thinkers solve problems of ends and of the relationship between ends and means, we need also to consider in some detail the characteristics of institutional theory in order to understand how political thinkers attempt to discover the ways in which structures come jointly to implement the values of the society. We have seen that political behaviour is constrained by structures, though we shall have to explore the implications of this constraint further.

We must also explore the relationship between behaviour and norms, as it is as obscure as that between structures and norms. Frequently behaviour reflects norms only in part, as political behaviour, like structures, has its own independent rules. The relationship between politicians over time creates a 'system' by which some of the actions of today are affected by yesterday's actions, irrespective of the norms of the polity. Alongside normative and institutional or structural theory, behavioural theory has therefore to discover and explain these semi-independent 'rules' governing behaviour. Overall, in political life, the influence of norms is at best indirect: it is cushioned and delayed. Even if one contends that, in some purely logical fashion, norms are paramount, the translation of the values into structures and into behaviour is such a complex process that, in practice, truly autonomous laws and principles have to be examined in the fields of structures and of behaviour.

Behaviour constitutes the flow of political life – the continuous element which, slowly or rapidly, helps to change the course of politics. It is thus the stuff of politics. Normative theory is highly abstract, in the sense that it is necessarily remote from what actually happens; only if values affect behaviour can normative theory be said to have its place in man's society and be more than a dream for some idealists. The relationship between norms and structures and between structures and behaviour not only provides a meeting point for political thinkers; it also provides a justification for those political thinkers who have hoped to remain on the normative plane. The circularity of the connections between norms, structures and behaviour is one of the important elements of the common concern of political thinkers.

To say that there is a common concern is not to deny the divisions in the approaches which we saw in the previous chapter. The autonomy of the sectors has meant that each has drawn upon the knowledge of different disciplines, and therefore contributed to the enrichment of political science. From history to law, from mathematics to philosophy, political thinking has received the support of men concerned with different levels of the same discipline. We have seen how the various sectors are united: in the attempt to define the object of study, and in the acceptance of the interrelationships between the lines of inquiry. There is recognition of a general idea of common ground – that of the heavy hand of the reality. All political analysis is shaped by the same constraints and by the realization of constraints: these constraints result from the ambiguous situation of man in society, his striving for an ideal and his recognition of his imperfections. We shall come up against the same constraints when we look at the methodology of political thinkers (the way in which they approach their task of identifying problems and examining the object of study).

CHAPTER 4

The methodology of political thinking

Political science is an eclectic discipline: the methodology used by political scientists is, of course, also eclectic. It is largely inherited from parent disciplines: political philosophers engage in arguments of a philosophical nature, as other philosophers; those who study the unique characteristics of events and statesmen work on documents with the same skills as historians; specialists of voting behaviour borrow from statistics the instruments with which to analyse evidence and come to conclusions; legal categories and a legal frame of mind is applied to the study of constitutions, institutions and structures; and those who attempt to apply to political life general models of behaviour draw, like economists, most of their techniques from mathematics. The discipline is ubiquitous: it should be, and is to a large extent, a market-place for techniques rather than the source of a coherent and integrated methodology.

At the level of techniques, it is therefore absurd to look for unity. Political scientists themselves would regard such an attempt as preposterous. They recognize the eclecticism of their discipline; they might indeed show much cynicism, or at least realism, about the power of various techniques, all of which up to now have been found wanting on one or another counts. All techniques have been criticized, partly because they have been imported and may better fulfil the needs of other disciplines than those of political science, partly because each approach has its limitations and each of the techniques corresponds to one of the approaches. As we said in Chapter 2, quantitative methods have been criticized because numbers cannot often be found in reality, and are thus artificially imposed. Documents are, of course, useful, but, in practice, access is often difficult and, even

when obtained, documents reveal only part of the story. Legal
categories are unsatisfactory and need to be modified in order to
go beyond descriptions of strictly legal structures to cover the
whole of society. Every technique is found wanting – even by the
very scholars who adhere to the corresponding approach. The
mathematically inclined political scientist sees that it is difficult
to apply mathematics to many of the problems that interest
him; historically minded students of politics recognize the
inadequacies of historical techniques in many aspects of their
inquiries.

A basic scepticism about techniques thus pervades the profession; most feel probably that it will never be possible to find a
satisfactory technique, in view of the diffuseness and complexity
of the discipline, while others, more sanguine or more idealistic,
hope that improvements will be made. The growth in the use of
mathematical models in the 1960s indeed corresponded to a
period when such 'optimists' increased; but these were also men
who had at times been disillusioned by the power of statistics
alone to meet the requirements of political analysis. The hope
was that a broader use of mathematics would lead to the construction of more plausible models of political life.

Yet, despite this diversity and this scepticism about techniques – indeed partly because of this scepticism – political
scientists tackle the problems which they wish to study on the
basis of an intellectual method which has common characteristics. If asked what they mean by liberty, how to assess power
in a committee, or the likely evolution of Western party
systems, political thinkers will adopt a broadly similar
methodological approach. There will be, first, a survey of the
problem and of the ways in which various concepts can be clari-
fied and made more precise; there will then be an attempt to
relate these concepts to others. There will thus be an effort at
comparing and contrasting, often designed to discover the
various elements which compose the concept or concepts under
analysis. The process is automatic and often instinctive, at least
for the broad mass of those who are engaged in political study;
but the training in the discipline consists precisely in acquiring
these skills and in gradually acquiring more assurance by being
able to establish more quickly certain comparisons and correlations – between ideas, facts and problems, whether norms,

structures or behaviour are the objects of study.

I.   *Classification and typologies*

Suppose a political scientist is confronted with the question of 'liberty'. He has, first, to try to give some preliminary meaning to this broad and very vague concept. Meaning suggests relationships. But it suggests also showing differences between varieties. Liberty means to 'be able to do what one wants', but one person wants many things at different times, so liberty must take many forms. *Some* measure of liberty can surely be assumed to exist everywhere; so one problem is to explore the *extent* of liberty, not just its presence or absence. This extent of freedom will be related (in fact or theory) to some situation, to some *liberties*. Differences between greater or lesser freedom, 'licence' *v.* freedom, will all connect back to the original concept. But an identical intellectual method will be used whether one looks at freedom from a 'descriptive' or a 'prescriptive' angle. Differences and relations have to be established whether one wants to see what kind of liberty exists in a country or whether one wants to show that freedom is an idea that should be cherished. Turning to reality to see what might be done, the student of politics will look at examples in which liberty or compulsion have been exercised or could have been exercised. A dialectic will begin to occur between this experience and the notions that arose out of the student's inquiry into the meaning of liberty.

It would seem appropriate at this point to explore further examples and categories. But this is preceded by the more demanding effort to relate these examples and categories. As the student of politics looks for examples, he is guided by some categories, but he makes his categories while he is assessing the strength of examples. Maybe the examples do not fit a concept which comes readily to mind: thus an unnamed problem remains in the open. Perhaps he has in mind a concept which does not seem easily buttressed by examples: thus he has to grapple with problems in a rather messy and inductive fashion.

How can he then proceed? He sees that there is, for instance, more or less liberty; he sees that he will have to be rather more precise about what licence is; he sees more and more cases (real or imagined, descriptive or prescriptive) where liberty, licence and compulsion show irregularities and give but little scope for simple analyses. To take freedom of expression, for instance; there are many types of expression, types of criticisms expressed, forms of language used, attacks against persons. And the same could be said about any freedom – of movement, of association, of assembly. Some freedoms seem innocuous, others seem quite dangerous, for one's self (suicide) or others (murder or theft); some seem 'positively loaded' (freedom of speech) but may be abused (incitement to murder through freedom of speech). None of these problems can be easily solved.

Outside normative questions similar difficulties confront those interested in understanding problems. How can one tackle the question of the future of Western party systems? In some cases there is apparent stability (U.K., Scandinavia), but also some discontent. Elsewhere, there may be stability, but it looks temporary and has the character of an uneasy truce, as in France since De Gaulle or as in Italy where the communist challenge seems a potential danger to traditional structures. Elsewhere, systems seem to be changing, as in Belgium, where the profound divisions within the parties are due to the linguistic cleavage between Walloons and Flemish; but there is also much change in nearby Netherlands, which cannot be explained by similar divisions.

Normative, institutional and behavioural analyses seem to produce very untidy categories: the first task then is to see how some type of order can be introduced into the messy landscape.

A. *Classification.* Before he can proceed more rigorously to the finding of the facts and the building of a conceptual analysis, the student of politics has to grapple with elements which do not lend themselves easily to being organized. His first step has to be to make piles, with no clear guidance, at the start, about the basic differences between the various piles. At times, he will have to undo the piles and start again; sometimes the elements will be divided into two piles, sometimes into more. Of course, as he gains experience on a given subject, some of these classifications will become clearer and more sophisticated; but when confronted with a new problem, his reaction will have to be mainly a leap in the dark.

Slowly, a better idea emerges of the criteria on which to classify. Part of the training is clearly an effort to shorten this process. As when stones are divided and put into piles, first simple criteria of outside appearance – size, colour, form – will come to be used. Similarly, liberty can be divided into freedoms to do certain things; party systems can be classified by the number of parties; members of a committee can be classified by the subjects on which they speak. But as there will always be more than one criterion, so there will be differences as to which criterion should come to be chosen: should the number of parties, or the type of programmes, or the type of leaders be the criterion by which to sort party systems? It is not sufficient to look for criteria, one has also to look for a 'criterion of criteria', a reason for applying a certain criterion rather than others. Much descriptive classification remains none the less at the first level of classification, as long as no 'reason' is discovered which ranks the criteria in terms of importance.

Many inquiries have of course gone further than simple classifications in a number of piles. But simple classification is still a common method for new inquiries. Unless good objective reasons suggesting otherwise immediately emerge from the subject itself, the 'instinct' will almost always be to look for the *dichotomies* or *trichotomies* which might be discovered. Hence political systems have often been divided into three categories, namely 'monarchies', 'oligarchies' and 'democracies', a division started by Aristotle which carried through the Middle Ages to the modern period. Party systems have been divided into 'single', 'two' and 'multi'. Regimes have been viewed as 'stable' or 'unstable'. Perhaps the subconscious opposition between good and bad, or between good, bad and indifferent, is the origin of this search for contrasts. When there is no clear reason for doing otherwise, when there is no experience of the problem and a new value, institution or type of behaviour comes to be studied, the most immediate technique is that of classification into dichotomies or trichotomies and thus obtaining a primary organization of the matter at hand.

B. *Typologies.* Classifications raise numerous problems. They are not intellectually satisfying, because the problem of the criterion of criteria makes for a permanent questioning of the classificatory scheme. Liberty can be divided into abstract and concrete rights, but is it the same thing as the division between individual and collective freedom? Does the number of parties reflect differences in organization or ideology? Thus the

number of criteria leads to the possible relationship between
these criteria. If it were possible to take all the criteria together
and use them, for instance, to show how the relationship between the number of parties, the programmes of these parties
and their type of leadership could lead to an overall distinction
between party systems, one would arrive at a classification
which would have the merit (the aesthetic merit almost) of
really covering the whole of the problem and thus avoiding the
question of the criterion of criteria. Political scientists have been
constantly looking for these comprehensive distinctions: they
sometimes stumbled on them by devising a *typology*, which is one
of the main ways of understanding the nature of what is being
classified.

A typology is the division of elements (normative or descriptive) into a number of related categories; ideally, the categories
would be the same whatever criteria were applied – in practice
one has to be satisfied if only *some* of the categories coincide.
Even in this less pure form, there are few successful typologies
which can be really said to explain reality. Yet Aristotle, Montesquieu and Marx, for instance, have devised typologies which
come very near to being successful.[1] If successful, typologies
come to be a 'proof' of what is being advanced. Whereas with
classifications one can never be sure that the criterion chosen is
truly important, and any criterion of criteria will almost certainly be rejected by some on a number of grounds, a typology
which brings all the criteria under one broad framework (in
statistical terms a high correlation between the 'variables') will
seem to constitute a proof that one really 'understands' or
grapples with reality. If divisions on freedom relate individual
freedoms to 'abstract' freedoms and collective freedoms to more
'concrete' freedoms, if party organization and party programmes coincide, the impression prevails that the distinction is
indeed of major importance. Thus Aristotle and Montesquieu
attempted to connect the points which they had made about the
three-fold distinction between political systems with some characteristics about human conduct and with a specific 'genius' of

[1] Aristotle's division between monarchy, oligarchy and democracy, which has
been echoed by Montesquieu, has the self-contained character of a typology,
as does Marx's division of societies into slave-based, feudal and bourgeois in
The Capital.

each of these systems.

C. *Typologies and the development of political life.* The typologies (and classifications) that we have mentioned are static, in the sense that they utilize fixed elements of systems, political parties of values. But typologies have also been important in describing successive phases of political development. Admittedly, typologies are not able to cover continuous aspects. This is a great drawback, which some forms of conceptualization of a more developed nature (to which we shall come later in this chapter) have tried – somewhat unsuccessfully – to remedy. But students of politics have always viewed their subject as being composed of discrete elements, as well as discrete changes. Some typologies have allowed for comparisons over time as well as space, as does that of Aristotle. Montesquieu was perhaps more concerned with time: to him the growth and decay of societies was organic. But the clearest case of a dynamic typology is of course that of Marx, who aimed specifically (because of his revolutionary hopes) to put forward reasons for one system necessarily evolving into another. In doing so, he did not create an intrinsically different typology from that of other thinkers; indeed he followed a series of evolutionary thinkers who saw political life and society as producing various epochs which altered the structure of society in a discrete way.[2]

Typologies are the backbone of political thinking. Almost all works of political science use either classifications or typologies – though the latter, despite their development, are often partial or contrived. It may seem to the outsider that this is not much to boast about – that political science is based on these constructs. But this would be to underestimate the importance of this method for the development of political analysis. It was not obvious when Aristotle suggested it (and it is still refuted by some) that regimes should be divided into 'autocracies, oligarchies and democracies'; it is no more obvious that the two-party system, together with other systems which have one large party, should be one of the most stable forms of parliamentary system.

[2] The notion of various stages in society was very common in the first half of the nineteenth century: it forms in particular the basis of much of the analysis of Auguste Comte (1798-1857) who in his *System of positive philosophy* claims that mankind had gone through theological, metaphysical and positive (i.e., scientific) ages.

In fact typologies have permeated from specialists to the public; they are of practical use: presumably one feels that some countries, because of their system, their freedom, or other characteristic, are acceptable, while others are rejected.

Admittedly, as micro-politics takes place within structures, it is less likely than macro-politics to be susceptible to typologies. And as practitioners are involved essentially in micro-politics, typologies are perhaps even more alien to them than to the political public. By making classifications – however rough – and then developing typologies, political scientists have gained a grip on reality; they have also managed to elucidate many political problems for others.

II.   *Surveying reality: examples, cases and case-studies*
We must return, however, to the point where the political scientist began considering examples, because the gathering of examples raises problems in a new area, for which a second basic methodology has been developed. Although autonomous, it is closely linked to the creation of typologies. Through the increased sophistication of examples, political scientists have often been drawn to the study of cases; they have begun to use a case-study method which is akin to that used in medicine or psycho-analysis.

A. *Examples*. We should examine the development of this methodology, because there is a controversy in political science over the extent to which case-studies should be employed. As we saw, all political scientists have been involved in the examination of examples. Examples are illustrative, of course, but they are also more important: they are part of the *demonstration* process in which political scientists are engaged, even if these do not always recognize it. This is because political scientists, whether they like it or not, are concerned with elements, with facts that impose certain constraints on them. Because facts are so important, examples cannot be just illustrative. Sooner or later, a critic within the discipline will undermine an argument on the grounds that the example given is not correctly assessed, or is not typical. Theories of electoral behaviour, now highly elaborate, stemmed from the gradual recognition of the inadequacy of random statements made by earlier political scientists about the likely attitudes of people to government. It is surely not sufficient to say that working class vote Labour because they are working class. Do they all do so? Is it exclusively because they are working class? Or for some other reason? What started as an example of the role of class (on which might be based some form of generalization or typology) has become the material for technical expertise.

The study of examples led to the improvement of techniques of analysis and has been the basis of the use of a large statistical apparatus in some important sub-fields of inquiry, specifically in voting and attitude studies. A one-line example necessitated tomes of survey results. Not all surveys have been justified on the grounds of a better determination of the character of examples, admittedly; surveys led to an increased use of quantitative techniques, which in turn led to the use of more mathematics and, thus, formal analyses became more widespread. A gradual development was seized upon by 'generalists' as of potential use. But, for a long time, sheer curiosity and the in-built pressures within the discipline led first to a search for examples, then for better examples, and produced major changes through the use of techniques. The convential historical document was in-adequate (though still the only means in many circumstances); hence came the reliance on forms of interviews (talks and discussions to begin with). Surveys came to be used as a more comprehensive and systematic set of interviews, though the development of this technique followed the statistical discovery that small samples could provide representative results. The luxurious growth of these techniques was rather an embar-rassment: what began as a method of study – the finding of examples to justify a conclusion – proved to be a large sub-section of the whole discipline, as if a very long tail had started wagging a rather small dog.

B. *Cases*. Another growth which developed accidentally out of the need for examples is the 'case'. The case is more than just an example in the ordinary sense, because it incorporates a number of characteristics – indeed a number of highly complex characteristics. If an example is given in passing it can be ambiguous: both illustrative and demonstrative. But when a complex technology of interviews or documents is involved, it suggests that the example must have a demonstrative role. Though it remains an example, the hope seems to be that a typology will be derived from it. By using cases, political scientists were admitting that reality was highly complex; a case, which is a three-dimensional picture of reality, can only be necessary if the situation is too complicated to be represented by examples.

Of course, the case-method derives from the historians' interest in unique events, or in great men; there, too, there is a desire to represent a situation globally. But cases are used much more widely in political science. A large number of problems are tackled in this way, to an almost surprising extent; even 'systematic' political thinkers will use cases, even if they are unique, to prove a point. Studies of political parties, of interest groups, of leaders' performance and of countries' development have been repeatedly made on the basis of cases, sometimes purely descriptive, often with a theory or a hypothesis.

While in fields such as political behaviour, the survey has played a major part and seemed to become the star child of the discipline, it is recognized that much of the work has been composed of particular cases; perhaps even a majority, though it is difficult to classify some borderline instances which are more historical narratives. One might dismiss this as a mere aberration on the part of scholars who are not aware of the needs for the discipline to be more systematic or formal, on the one hand, or more normative on the other. The cases often are not rigorous enough to prove a point, or, on the other hand, are too one-sided to be considered truly historical. The tools of such studies are of course improving all the time, and they are in effect borrowed from other disciplines; still, reality is so complex that it sometimes defies reduction to one simple example.

C. *Case-studies*. An effort has been made by the use of case-studies to combine both a proof of generalization and a description of events. This is possible only if there is repetition of broadly similar types. Thus, while cases may aim at studying big events, organizations or leaders, case-studies have to concentrate on much smaller events. A typical case study would be in the field of policy-making, such as education or housing, where many authorities have similar problems or even the same authority has to be much involved.

Suppose that one wants to try to see a pattern emerging in the way in which decisions are taken; suppose that, for instance, one would like to pile in different categories various types of decisions from different bodies of the same type (for instance of local authorities) or from the same body over time or in different areas (in education or in housing) in order to assess whether there are differences between various forms of decision-making or various forms of power exercised by committee members (i.e. if a typology can be supported). There is a great temptation to arbitrarily categorize decisions which do not readily simplify. If one is to study decisions about municipal housing, for instance, it becomes necessary to know how the matter was put forward (was it originated by one member of the town council, by a political party, by a pressure group and, especially, by a 'housing activist group' created *ad hoc*?). How did the matter come to the town council? Was the process slow or rapid? What was the outcome? One must describe the decision in detail, relate it to the pressure put at the beginning and see how quickly and how far it was implemented. In order to produce a typology, the description must be as exhaustive and precise as possible.

But, because we want to classify decisions, we need to use instruments which are comparable. There is nothing to classify if the study is not exhaustive, but there is no means of classification unless the same criterion or criteria are used from the outset: hence very tricky problems of technical arrangements. The more one tries to find precise criteria, the less is it possible to retain the concrete characteristics of the reality; the broader the field of the intended case study, the more problems there are. Many individual and collective efforts have been made to use case-studies to classify countries.[3] Their lack of success has resulted either from being too concrete (and therefore being a series of disconnected examples) or from being too abstract (and having little flavour of the reality).

We can now appreciate the dilemma: examples lead inexorably to complex descriptions, which have to be complex to be realistic and become more complex by trying to relate fact and analysis. Yet this is a problem which students of politics cannot

[3] Many studies have been conducted on a 'parallel' basis, for instance between countries; here a series of cases are analysed, hopefully according to the same criteria. This is sometimes done within a particular work. G. A. Almond has, for instance, edited his first comparative work, *The Politics of the Developing Areas* (Princeton U.P., Princeton, 1960), in collaboration with J. S. Coleman, on the basis of this principle.

avoid – and know they cannot avoid. They have to classify the manifestations of reality; they have to look for manifestations in order to ensure that their ideas do indeed correspond to reality; they have to subject these manifestations to careful examination as they need to be sure that they can place them in one of their piles. Some may choose to reject the method, but such a decision is difficult to hold for more than a short period.

III.   *Concepts and the search for the continuous*

Typologies constitute a half-way house between pure generalization and a wholly random examination of reality. They are only a first step towards an analysis of a situation. If political scientists find that the facts of an individual case do not lend themselves to a typology, then the classification approach will not be applicable. On the other hand, typologies themselves make discrete links between the elements of the case and are only an in-between stage between induction and deduction. In the process of classification, if a criterion does not naturally emerge, then a logical justification for the choice of criterion must be made. Conceptualization takes place alongside the inductive process.

Classifications and typologies can lead to simplified contrasts, often based on dichotomies, as we saw; this is why concepts are more likely to be used. It seems both more logical and at times empirically more justifiable to attempt to consider reality and indeed any problem by continuous dimensions and incremental variations. This, of course, goes against the constant reminder constituted by the existence of structures which seem to be, and indeed are, discrete. It may be that a typology with sharp divisions will correspond more closely to the reality; but only successful typologies will be entirely satisfactory in this regard; the distinction must go beyond a mere classification which the researcher might have superimposed. If no empirical evidence suggests divisions, and if a deductive approach is attempted, then continuous elements will be taken into consideration.

A. *The problem of the definition of concepts.* Political phenomena and ideas have long been characterized by abstract concepts; the first concepts to be introduced were drawn directly from normative approaches; they related to principles designed to

affect conduct: notions of liberty, equality, oligarchy or democracy. When these concepts were applied (or some efforts were
made to apply them), they lost the wholly normative basis they
had originally and came to be used in descriptive analyses.
These concepts were often at first viewed – and sometimes still
are – as describing or suggesting clearly definable situations. We
discussed liberty as potentially giving rise to dichotomies; democracy was viewed by Aristotle, and many successive thinkers,
as one element in a trichotomy. Gradually, however, many of
these concepts came to be used in various situations; the fact
that they were rarely implemented – or at least in full – led to
them being considered as concepts in more general and theoretical analysis.

This was probably helped by the development of a second
type of concept, more neutral or at least originally more descriptive, designed to account for the internal mechanics of political systems. The oldest and possibly most common is that of
legitimacy, which emerged from the idea of legality, but became
distinct as problems of politics were separated from problems of
law and came to include questions of enforcement and acceptance. A number of other concepts which have become common
have similar aims, though their origin is more directly political:
the concept of power, in particular, as well as concepts such as
influence, compulsion and authority, has been central to the
large literature purporting to explain individual decisions and
the maintenance of systems. More recently, under the influence
of economics, concepts such as exchange, trade-off or bargaining have come to be applied to political situations. Increasingly,
and consciously, the use of concepts has thus helped to give a
more formal base to political analysis.

Yet these concepts raised in the past and continue to raise
problems of definition. The archetypal controversy is over
'power': some have been deterred from using the concept because it has raised such major difficulties.[4] A pure deductive

[4] This is not the place to enter the major controversy which the concept of
power raised as there have been numerous definitions, which do not wholly
overlap. For a summary of the controversy and a general comment of one of
the contemporary authors who has been most involved in the theoretical study
and the attempts at operational measurement, see R. A. Dahl, 'Power', *International Encyclopaedia of the Social Sciences*, vol. 12.

method never seems wholly tenable; questions of fact and past classifications and typologies cannot be totally ignored in making definitions. Concepts may be used in order to achieve general distinctions of a continuous kind, but, almost automatically, the need for realism quickly re-emerges, mainly because of two difficulties which are at the root of many controversies: first, the relationship between concepts; second, questions of measurement, or, to put it differently, the relationship between concepts and possible indicators.

B. *The relationship between concepts.* Suppose that a political scientist suggests some definitions of concepts and postulates relationships between them: criticisms will soon be raised, ostensibly about the definition of the concepts, more profoundly about the relationships between these concepts. These criticisms occur because no political scientist is prepared to determine a number of postulates and corollaries wholly *a priori* without paying at least some attention to reality. Concept-building in political science bears a certain resemblance to cartography. Maps represent the earth: they represent the earth fairly accurately if they cover a limited area, but not if they correspond to a large area. If political scientists decided boldly to adopt entirely *a priori* definitions of concepts and built a deductive theory from these concepts, problems of definition and of relationships between definitions would not arise: concepts would cover what political scientists would have decided; relationships would be stipulated. Controversies would only occur over the extent to which the theorems which might follow would have been truly proven, or over the relationships between the theory and the reality.

This is not the normal process in political science, nor in other sciences either; but other sciences have been luckier (at least the natural sciences and to some extent economics) in stumbling on concepts which were both amenable to deduction *and* at least broadly corresponded to the reality (in that they led to a reasonably large number of valid predictions). In political science, a deductive theory has not been constructed, at least in general terms, largely because the narrower attempts that have been made floundered on problems of prediction. The rules of deductive theory have therefore been bent (in practice, and somewhat unconsciously), and concepts are not defined without some consideration for reality. No political scientist is ready to *postulate* relationships between concepts without empirical reference. But this has made controversies inevitable: scholars differ as to which 'map' should be considered accurate.

C. *The problem of measurement.* Since concepts are never defined independently from reality, problems of measurement necessarily arise. They arise at two levels. First, and perhaps paradoxically, they arise precisely because concepts are never designed without considering the 'shape' of the reality. If power is defined, for instance, as 'the relationship by which A makes B do something which he would otherwise not do', this definition covers many situations when it is common for the public to use the word 'power'. But this leads to controversies about the extent to which power manifests itself in a particular case. We move from the concept – high, clear and abstract – to the problems of facts, cases and history. If a definition was adopted *a priori*, corollaries deduced, and theorems proved, it might be possible to see whether or not reality did fit, in the end, with the model produced. But as concepts correspond only to those situations currently being considered, they can only correspond to part of all possible situations. Thus they always leave some room for controversy about the real nature of particular cases.

Second, since concepts remain close to reality, the need becomes pressing to find indicators in order to come to conclusions about the reality. A definition of power is therefore followed by an effort to see, for instance, whether behaviour in a committee can help to measure differences between the power of participants in decisions taken. But continuous indicators are difficult to find. The broader they are, the more controversies emerge about whether they 'really' correspond to the problem stated. Are stable governments indicators of stable regimes? Is the regime more stable in direct and linear proportion to the stability of the government? The choice of indicators corresponds in reality to a choice of concepts and to a relationship between concepts, since indicators are concepts of a narrower kind selected because they are held to represent – and thus to be associated with – the parent concept which is being studied. The reasons which lead to a lack of agreement on concept relationships also lead to a lack of agreement on the relationship between concepts and indicators. The effort to discover general concepts becomes frustrated and every generation of students of politics continues to be worried – or may become increasingly worried – about the usefulness of developing new concepts and of linking these concepts in a deductive theory.

Thus conceptualization leads to more than just some difficulties: it leads apparently to an impasse, at least if pushed too far away from typologies and classifications. The development of concepts is part of the dialectic opposing 'discrete' and 'incremental' elements, both of which exist in the field itself; this dialectic is reflected in the mind of almost everyone who thinks politically. The conflict is unavoidable: it might be solved, one day, if a predictive deductive theory were to be devised, but this will only happen if the state of formal theory improves dramatically, if the nature of structures is much better understood and if mathematical techniques become less closely linked to a numerical base. These conditions may be fulfilled, but as long as they are not the political scientist's mind will naturally swing between general concepts and classifications; with both an obsession for a good grip on the facts and a realization that facts must be organized if they are to be understood.

So we can see that there is a methodology common to political scientists, but that there are vast difficulties and frustrations involved. When confronted with a problem, the political scientist will 'know what to do', at least in the first instance, if he wants to isolate a subject of inquiry and attempt to tackle it. However, he will recognize that his methods are not likely to suffice, that it will be necessary to proceed by trial and error and that the choice might be between exaggerated empiricism, untestable generalizations or a much less intellectually satisfying middle way where much of the procedure will be based on forms of intuitive induction of a hazardous character.

Yet the subject has to proceed in this messy fashion, because of the nature of the questions which have to be solved. Too concrete to be content with generalizations, too abstract and general (too anxious to explain and to compare) to be content with descriptions of unco-ordinated examples, political science thus shapes the minds of those who engage in it in a very broad, eclectic, and, hopefully as a result, rich manner. I have tried up to now to show – indeed very much in the manner of the political scientists – how the divisions coexist in an uneasy unity. But we have as a result only scratched the surface of the arguments and problems which concern scholars in the discipline. It is now possible to go further into the details of these problems and these difficulties. For this, however, we need to examine separately the three branches of the discipline: normative, structural and behavioural. By surveying each of these, we will have occasion to see how far the constraints of reality and idealism, of detailed analysis and generalization, constitute both intractable problems and a challenge, giving the discipline its *raison d'être* and its intellectually stimulating character.

PART II

The Three Branches of Political Thinking

CHAPTER 5

Normative Theory

We have now a general idea of the problems which political thinkers face and of the tools that they can use. We can therefore have a closer look at the way they approach and conduct their investigations. Let us start by those who are concerned with the goals of society, the normative thinkers. They are interested in understanding, not how or why society works, but the values that should be pursued. They may feel that there is not enough liberty, or not enough justice, in the country in which they live, or in the world in general. They may want to solve apparent contradictions between goals, or indeed stemming from the same goal: the freedom of one individual may limit that of others, for instance; what then should be the limits of individual freedom? How do we solve the dilemma between freedom and equality?

But normative thinkers are not only interested in discovering a 'package of goals' for themselves: they want to influence others. They have therefore to make a convincing case. To do so, they must use logic; but they must also be, at least in part, empirical. There might be a theoretical case for greater liberty or greater equality; but these ideals may not be viable in practice beyond a certain point. Normative theorists must therefore be concerned with the links between their proposals and day-to-day experience.

I. *The starting point of the normative inquiry*
   A. *The organization and ranking of values.* The normative thinker starts his inquiry because he wishes to explore moral and political values. But where does he get these values from? It is surely not the case that he 'invents' them; moral and political values

are largely given to him by the world around him. In relation to
the broad spectrum of moral and political goals, the theorist is
more like an 'organizer' than a 'creator'.

Since the values exist, not merely in the mind of the political
thinker, but in the minds of many other thinkers of the past and
present, and, indeed, in the minds of many men and women
around him, they are *facts* with which the normative theorist has
to contend and which he must treat exactly in the same way as
facts are treated, for instance, by descriptive political theorists.
Unlike the poet or the artist, the normative thinker cannot
altogether originate his material: a number of broad concepts
are passed from one generation to the next, such as freedom,
equality, justice and responsibility. Also, these concepts are
already implemented in society, through various freedoms,
various types of equality, various forms of justice. If the normative theorist is to have influence, he has to take these values and
the manifestations of these values into account.

But, it may be argued, the normative theorist can at least
select among these facts: he may emphasize liberty more than
equality; he may discuss only responsibility or justice. But the
theorist must justify his choice by argument: it is not obvious
that equality should be preferred to liberty; and if the theorist is
to be convincing, the case must be argued strongly and per-
suasively.

The main task of the normative thinker therefore is not to list
moral and political values – this has already been done; nor is it
to select one or more values and concentrate on them; it is to
organize and rank these values. Perhaps he will develop a
hierarchy of goals; or a new general principle for reorganizing
the various goals. This is what a truly satisfactory normative
theory can hope to achieve. But goals are so numerous and often
so conflicting that some may be abandoned in the analysis; such
exclusionism must result in a loss of credibility.

One can therefore discern three distinct elements in the normative thinkers' approach to the problems they study. One is a
truly *personal* element. It is of course difficult to define precisely
the extent of the purely personal: some have even suggested that
we are entirely the product of our environment. But surely there
is something idiosyncratic in the way we organize our views –
and therefore some idiosyncratic aspect in the way in which

normative thinkers adopt and rank values. But a more important point is that the intellectual arguments are in fact strongly
influenced by effective reactions to moral and political values.
Even the words used are emotionally loaded: liberty and
equality, for instance. Some normative thinkers, like Hobbes,
advocate peace at all costs, finding violence and disorder particularly repellent. Others, like Marx, are most concerned to erase
inequality and oppression; violence and disorder are simply less
worrying to them than the continuation of exploitation.

But we are already moving from purely personal factors to the
role of *experience*. Political thinkers are surrounded by political
events: happenings of various kinds affect their values and become intertwined with the emotional reactions that we have just
described; they also lead to reflections about the relative importance of values. A thinker who believes that equality should
be overriding will have his view reinforced if he sees that 'rug-
ged' individual liberty leads to the maintenance of slums and
other forms of social squalor while a few can live a 'good life'
without State interference or government attempts at redistri-
bution. Empirical experience in social, economic, cultural or
scientific fields may also influence political attitudes; for
example, the discovery of nuclear fission might lead to conclusions that the power of leaders should be controlled by democratic processes. As political thinkers are more interested in
matters political than ordinary citizens, they are more likely to
be on the lookout for what happens, and thus to be affected by
experience. Of course, experience may be counterbalanced by a
deep-rooted prejudice or by subjective feelings; some political
theorists may reject or repress the experience of the world
around them if it does not fit the beliefs that they happen to
hold. But it is difficult to remain unaffected by events such as
wars, or personal crises, whether good or bad.

Meanwhile, political scientists are affected – significantly
more than other people – by the knowledge of an intellectual
tradition in the study of values. There is thus some development
in the sub-field of political science concerned with values: the
thinker cannot ignore altogether the views of Hobbes or Rousseau; for instance the problems which these authors tackled,
and therefore the values which they upheld and to which they
gave prominence. The development is not linear; it is not

'scientific'; it differs even possibly from developments in other parts of the discipline. Progress, if there is any, is dialectical; there is a cyclical element because political writers go in and out of fashion with contemporary political theorists. But some accumulation of knowledge, of approach, and of relationships between concepts does take place. The existence of a body of literature enables political scientists to avoid repeating discussions and thus to be 'educated' more quickly to problems of values.

These three types of influences cannot be clearly distinguished in the works of any particular thinker, or even any particular standpoint taken by a thinker on a problem. Authors are often quoted by others: Aristotle, Hobbes, Rousseau and Marx have played a considerable part and are frequently mentioned; but there are many subtle ways in which they influence those who come after them, even if no mention is made of their works. The pessimistic approach to politics can be termed 'Hobbesian' as Hobbes did originate a depiction of the relationship between men and society in which the inner drives of mankind are only checked by civil government. Rousseau's portrayal of society was optimistic, as he believed in man's capability for progress and thought problems occurred primarily because society was ill-organized, not because man was intrinsically 'bad'. These representations are part of the culture of every political thinker; they contribute to the elaboration of typologies, or at least of classification, in the same way as the Marxist typology contributes to socio-political typologies of political change. They shape the perception of the events; they can be used to rationalize emotions, but they also influence political thinkers to abandon, perhaps, or at least tone down some rationalizations. It would be an interesting intellectual exercise (perhaps profitable, but also highly complex) to attempt to assess precisely the extent to which these influences are intertwined in a particular political thinker, which of them tends to prevail, and the areas in which each prevails.

B. *The relationship between values and influences on attitudes to values.* As we said earlier, political values are in large part objects which the normative thinker has to treat as facts of some importance: the concepts of liberty and equality are givens; but, as we also said, he can – and has to – organize these values. What part do emotions, experience and tradition play in this process? The impact of tradition is unquestionably greatest in the identification of the subject-matter (the isolation of values) while the empirical environment and emotions are most influential on the line taken by the thinker about the rankings given to these values.

Since the values that need to be discussed – liberty, equality, justice, for instance – cannot be deduced directly from an overriding principle as in mathematics, the works of other writers are often the substitute for straightforward logic. This may mean that political scientists no longer have the resolve, boldness or naïvety to hope to be able to reconstruct the principles on which mankind should base its political actions. The absence of a satisfactory deductive theory leads to a permanent desire to start again from first principles, since none of the previous theories have solved all problems. But, at the same time, the relative failure of previous generations makes new thinkers sceptical about their potential for success in such an enterprise. So the landscape of principles tends to be determined by the way in which previous thinkers have ordered it.

Emotional and empirical factors are more influential in the determination of the line taken by political thinkers. Every political thinker has a basic feeling for liberty or equality. Indeed, those who become concerned with these questions do so because of emotional drives to structure principles in a different way from previous generations; they are affected, for instance, by the picture of injustice throughout the world in its many different and new forms. Hobbes was concerned (perhaps obsessed) by disorder and civil war in the world around him. Nineteenth-century socialist thinkers came to feel the need for equality, because of the industrial conditions in Western Europe at the time. The discovery that social-democratic reformism did not lead (or no longer led) to major changes in Western society after the 1950s may have induced some thinkers to re-evaluate the role of revolution, and to play down the role of peace.[1]

[1] This is clearly at the root of much of the 'critical' rethinking of liberal society which has taken place in the U.S. and elsewhere in the West, in particular since the second half of the 1960s. For an example of this approach, see L. Strauss, *What is Political Philosophy* (Free Press, New York, 1959).

Yet this tendency for emotional and empirical considerations to dominate the attitude on values and for the intellectual tradition to be a guideline to the 'landscape' is no more than a trend. Political thinkers of the past do influence future generations by the way they translated their emotions into their works; some emotions have become as a result 'impossible' or at least difficult to hold, while others are seemingly more 'acceptable'. The forcefulness with which Hobbes and Marx stressed the cases for order and for social equality respectively had a considerable impact on countless political thinkers. The notion of constraint, which we discussed in Chapter 3, can be seen to be implied by a pessimism about human nature: here again is the influence of a classical theory.

The process works the other way, too: the interpretation of principles – not in their broadest sense, but in their more specific sense – adapts to the emotional and empirical climate. For example, when Aristotle propounded his notion of 'democracy' as being government by all and for all, he did not include those who were enslaved; nowadays it would be inconceivable not to include them. With changes in attitudes to human relations, the concept of equality came to be regarded as inconsistent with slavery. Developments in the meaning of freedom, particularly to include concrete freedoms, and a concentration on conditions necessary to achieve those freedoms arose from disillusionment with the French and American revolutions. The type of freedom they declared was of little benefit to the mass of the population which was too poor, too ill-educated, and physically too exhausted to benefit from it.[2]

The development of values has thus to be seen as a blend of various sources leading to a given panorama of principles and of attitudes to these principles. So, contrary to first impressions, normative theory proves to be 'messy' and diffuse, confounding

[2] The distinction is sometimes made between freedom 'of' (thought, discussion, etc.) and freedom 'from' (want, unemployment, etc.). There has clearly been an increase in the influence of those who favour the latter type of freedom in the course of the twentieth century. See Bean and Peters, *op. cit.*, pp. 211 and ff. Among the first major critiques of the American Revolution in terms of it not establishing 'real' freedom for 'all' is the well-known study of C. Beard, *An economic interpretation of the Constitution of the United States* (Macmillan, London, 1913).

the hopes of those thinkers who seek to provide a definitive analysis and of those students who look for rigorous political guidance. The intellectual origins of normative theory are obscure and confused; they include the varied experiences of individual thinkers grappling with a reality which all too often cannot be reduced to a few categories. We recognize here the common dilemma facing political scientists, eager – or at least prone – to generalize but always brought back to the difficulties of accounting for situations they are faced with.

The origins of normative theory must be demystified – but this demystification should lead neither to scepticism nor, particularly, to easy criticism. We might wish to find something neater, simpler or more logical; but who would dare to say that, in the same circumstances as those political thinkers, we would have produced anything different?

II.   *The process of development of normative theory*
Let us now turn to the intellectual process by which those who think politically give some shape to their analyses, and gradually elaborate their blueprints for the 'good society'. These blueprints must be intellectually satisfying to the thinkers; they must also be convincing to readers. It might be argued that all political writers are proselytizing, and that even empirical theorists are engaged in convincing others of their viewpoint; but normative thinkers are especially missionary, since they want to ensure that society moves in the direction which they think is right. They have therefore to undertake, sequentially, and more commonly in combination, three different operations. First, they must elaborate their attitude to their preferred principles and in particular resolve the contradictions that might exist between the various values. Second, they must evaluate the society around them in the light of these values: if they want to see these values implemented, they must discuss how far contemporary society already embodies them, if at all. Third, they must take into account the 'potential' of mankind to implement their principles or these might never be put into practice.

A. *The elaboration of a system of principles.* The first step in the process of elaboration of a normative theory consists in a clarification of the various 'values': the stones have to be cleaned, so to speak, before they can be organized in piles. The process of classification must explore all the possible links between concepts; also the most extreme positions have to be considered. Is individual liberty to be allowed in *all* circumstances? Examples must be given of these circumstances. Whatever his beliefs or experiences, the thinker needs to use arguments – often drawn from tradition – to present a coherent system of principles.

Conflicting values, which prevent the discovery of an overriding principle, have to be tackled with straightforward logic. If the thinker believes in equality as the supreme principle for governing society, then he must deal with the conflicting claims of liberty; either he must prove that liberty is not as important in all circumstances, or that it is implied in equality. The political thinker is now confronted with an intellectual constraint: the fact that others have discussed liberty becomes a constraint to be paid attention to, if the model based on equality is to stand up.

At this point, many may simply say: why should political theorists be searching for an overriding principle? Why claim – almost at all costs – that equality is *the* end to follow? Is it not unrealistic to refuse to see that there are constraints due to other values, and indeed that *several* principles may be equally important? Why not approach the problem by saying, 'Here we have liberty and equality: these are two mutually exclusive concepts, at least if pushed to extremes, since if I leave A entirely free he may come to diminish the status of B to his benefit. Let me therefore look at different situations and define a "package of liberty and equality". I would find it very difficult to go outside this package either because liberty would be sacrificed to equality or because equality would be sacrificed to liberty.'

Normative thinkers do not approach the problems in this way. They come to constraints in passing, almost reluctantly. They do not usually wish to optimize: to weigh up the advantages and disadvantages of two goals in order to devise a combination incorporating the best characteristics of each. They are not neutral to principles, values or ends. One can optimize both liberty and equality only if one really values these two principles equally and if one thinks that some combination of the two will actively produce the best, or at any rate least bad system. Political thinkers typically start from the opposite point of view, usually because they want to promote *one* particular principle;

they start from the notion that one principle is essential, whether it be peace, liberty or equality. Moreover, they often seem to have a 'Manichean' view of society which may well be unconscious. Their aim is to show that one principle is to be extolled, because the opposite of that principle is bad. A recognition of intellectual constraints to the theory emerges therefore typically *during* the process of analysis, either because of prospective dangers inherent in a theory based exclusively on one principle or because there are contradictions within that principle (as we saw in the case of liberty).

So even when normative thinking begins as a desire to promote one value above all others, the next step consists in an attempt to harmonize and reconcile various values: one way of doing this is to suggest that all other values derive from, or are contained in, the overriding principle. Frequent attempts are made to show that 'real' liberty implies equality or that the liberty of the whole makes for the greater liberty of the individuals. Rousseau's notion that 'men should be forced to be free' comes close to this point of view. Such efforts epitomize the lengths to which political thinkers will go to avoid presenting problems of constraints as neat sums, as in economics. This may be criticized as 'unrealistic' – as indeed it is – but it is part of the 'tightrope' predicament of political science to be both realistic and unrealistic.

In the end, thinkers often *combine* the values which are discussed around them: this is their concession to realism. But if all their discussions were on this plane, normative theorists would prevent themselves from discussing the possible arrangements for different situations, for instance, if society held different values, or men had different aims. They would effectively prevent any such change from happening if they did not even discuss the possibility that these changes might occur. It is not lack of awareness or of logic that drives normative theorists to order values in ways that relegate constraints to a secondary role. Perhaps a different organization of society could lead to some *new* conciliation between these principles. The search for a good society must include endeavours towards such a conciliation.

B. *The evaluation of the current society.* The second (analytical) aspect of the process of normative thinking consists in

evaluating current society in the light of the system of principles
that has been elaborated. Such an evaluation involves the
familiar combination of descriptions and value-judgements
which characterizes all political thinking. The process of 'abs-
traction from reality' which the normative theorist applies is of
course informed by his experience. But even though the description and evaluation of the current society is often brief – at
times sweeping – it is essential to the discourse of the political
thinker, and it needs to be systematic. It may distinguish between various types of social and political systems, in order to
show that some are better than others – a distinction which in
turn might indicate that man could 'do better'. Whether the
thinker concludes that 'man is everywhere in chains' (Rousseau)
or that the Chinese cultural revolution suggests hope at least for
some aspects of today's society, he will still have to use the
descriptive-cum-evaluative statement about society.

There would be little need to mention this point were it not for
the fact that some – indeed many – evaluations of society consciously or unconsciously lie behind discussions of principle.[3] Of
course, it may happen that the thinker concentrates on discussing the 'good society' and aims at producing a utopia without
bothering about the characteristics of reality; but, even in this
case, the fact that he is concentrating on building a utopia implies some judgement of current society; if things were perfect,
there would be little point in building the utopia. Admittedly,
there may be cases when the thinker concentrates on discussing
the logical implications of concepts and engages in pure linguistic analysis – and thus appears remote from any desire to
evaluate. The analysis of concepts and of their interrelationships is indeed logically distinct from the evaluation of society;
but such an analysis is parasitic on broader works of normative

[3] See Chapter 3, p. 52, footnote 5, for a number of examples of such 'hidden'
statements. One contemporary example in the same vein can be given from H.
Marcuse's 'Liberation from the affluent society', in *The dialectics of liberation*, D.
Cooper, ed. (Penguin Books, Harmondsworth, 1968), p. 366: 'The subjective
need is repressed, again on a dual ground: firstly by virtue of the actual
satisfaction of needs and, secondly, by a massive scientific manipulation and
administration of needs – that is, by a systematic social control, not only of the
consciousness, but also of the unconsciousness of man.' All these statements
are 'empirical', yet the evidence is not given – and the need to give evidence
does not even appear to be felt!

theory. Its impact is at best indirect – to shake the conceptual foundations of studies which do place their main emphasis on the evaluation of society.[4]

The broad character of evaluations of current society made by normative theorists has been the cause of the criticisms stressed by more empirical political scientists who contend, with much supportive evidence, that the generalizations of normative theorists are unwarranted and are often so vague as to be difficult to prove or disprove. Normative theorists often resort to images or analogies which may have a high poetic content but do not support close analysis. But empirical political scientists also generalize when, as they often do, they pass judgements on the societies which they analyse: this has led to the counter-criticism of normative theorists who claim that, since only minutely detailed analyses can be rigorous, a purely 'empirical approach' will always be of limited value, as it does not enable us to pass the general judgements on societies which are needed for the task of improving the social condition of man.

C. *The 'potential' capabilities of mankind.* The evaluation of society as it is must be qualified by an evaluation of potential capabilities of mankind in a different society. Supposing that it were agreed that several principles should be upheld in the governing of society, but it were found that in contemporary society only a few of them were implemented: one still has to ask, what is the 'potential' of mankind? Can man be 'improved' and, if so, to what extent? Those normative theorists who, having evaluated society, come to the conclusion that society is 'good' or 'adequate' need not be concerned with man's 'potential', although they need to show that society (broadly) embodies the principles which they uphold (and they may be subjected to the counter-argument that society could be better). But normative thinkers who are not content with the *status quo* have to be concerned directly with what man could do as well as with what man does. Either they think that society is bad (or gets a low rating judged by their standards), or they feel that the fault lies with man himself. If the latter, they conclude that society

[4] Linguistic analysis has always been particularly developed in Britain, under the influence of the 'Oxford school' of 'positivism'. One very successful example is T. D. Weldon, *The Vocabulary of Politics* (Penguin Books, Harmondsworth, 1953).

cannot reasonably be expected to improve. If they believe man's potential to be greater, then a change in societal arrangements could enable him to adhere somewhat more closely to the hierarchy of values that they feel should be upheld. There may even be intermediate positions, such as those of theorists who judge man's potential to depend greatly on an education process: if the conditions under which man lived were different, man might be able to realize his potential more fully and thus eventually produce a better society. Whatever line is taken, as soon as society is viewed as not being 'perfect' (and few normative theorists have ever believed that it was, or are likely to do so in the future), it becomes necessary to discuss the potential of man.

From this need to explore the basic potential of mankind follow analyses of a dubious 'scientific' character. They are unavoidable. Political scientists are caught in a process which leads to inquiries into problems for which there can be no satisfactory solution, because they have to be based on a distinction between mankind and society which cannot be tested empirically; comments made in this area are necessarily hypothetical. Thus this type of analysis is always peculiarly semi-empirical, semi-imaginative (perhaps truly poetic). Help is sought from comparisons or evaluations of a somewhat mythical character or from little-known societies geographically or historically remote. Not surprisingly, normative theorists are led to examine the nature of the 'noble savage' or end up discussing the 'golden age'.[5] The fact that such 'good' societies are held to have existed in the past or to exist elsewhere gives a seemingly empirical basis for the view that society *can* be organized differently – better, according to the principles held by the theorist. If no example can be given of such a 'better' society in the past, either the normative theorist has to resort to believing in the virtues of education (and use as his empirical foundation some experiments at educating relatively small groups of children or adults living a 'communal' life); or he has to concede that man is not

[5] The notion of the 'noble savage' was particularly prevalent in the second half of the eighteenth century, though it is not always clear whether this Golden Age was deemed to have existed or not: this ambiguity exists, for instance, with Rousseau. But an obsession with the past can be found among political theorists in almost every generation.

really potentially better than society – and has to adopt a 'realistic' viewpoint.[6] He may then go as far to the opposite extreme as Hobbes and suggest that man is in fact potentially worse than society; that it is through some form of civil government that man's 'base' instincts can be tamed.

While the description and evaluation of current societies borrows from the historical side of empiricism in political analysis, the examination of the potential of mankind very often comes close to asserting a number of 'laws' about human nature. These 'laws' are often assumed without conscious recognition, possibly because a conscious recognition that such laws were asserted would force normative theorists to realize that these laws were not proven and were at best very difficult to prove; theorists might therefore become bogged down in complex empirical analyses which would distract them from their main goal, which is to press for the implementation of the system of values which they uphold. Yet these laws *are* presented and the point must be noted, even if this entails remarking on the somewhat dubious practice of those authors of asserting laws without even warning readers that they are, at best, unproved hypotheses. Hobbes and Marx are perhaps the only two political theorists who rigorously established their underlying premises, though even they cannot be said to have 'proved' their case. But the assertion of laws of mankind is extremely common in the literature; a systematic analysis would unquestionably reveal – devastatingly for many authors – how much of normative theory is dependent on these unproved hypotheses.[7]

Can normative theorists be justified in using so loosely types of reasoning which go much beyond their original brief? They aim to analyse the goals of society and to propose the best possible goals for mankind; in the process, they come to pass

[6] The idea of 'education' is at the root of much of left-wing thinking in relation to possible changes of man, and explains why it is suggested that such guardians as, for instance, the Communist Party have to be created, at least for a period. This is reflected in the views currently held in many parts of the Third World and, especially, in Mao's China and Castro's Cuba.

[7] It is not possible here to go into a detailed analysis of texts, but the examples which were given in Chapter 3, pp. 35/6 and in the footnote of that page give an idea of the type of generalizations which are made and on which normative theory is dependent if it is to be convincing and have a practical impact.

sweeping judgements on existing societies and on the potential of mankind. Logically, no justification is possible; indeed, it is hoped that normative theorists will appreciate the need for a more solid empirical basis – a basis at least as solid as that of Hobbes or Marx (which were firmly grounded considering the state of the social sciences in their time). But, as we saw, only by examining the existing society and the nature of man can one propose any change. The ability of normative theorists to convince others (and themselves) about change depends on establishing a link between values, society and man. Many normative thinkers are unquestionably carried away by their desire to convince others; but the predicament is unavoidable.

One cannot simply list a number of values, possibly reconcile them, turn them into an overall blueprint for society, and then abandon the matter at this point, leaving readers and political leaders to sort out whether these principles and this blueprint can be implemented. It is the function of political scientists to try to show what values can be implemented and in what way. The endeavours of normative political theorists are thus not only difficult, but unrewarding in contrast with the aesthetic pleasure that a mathematician may take in deductive constructions. The problems posed by normative analyses provide further evidence both of the diffuseness of political science and of its challenging character.

III.   *The end-products of normative theory: utopias and ideologies*
One may justifiably criticize normative theory either on the grounds of its lack of empirical bases or on the grounds of its internal disagreements; yet normative thinkers fulfil a much-needed role in society, having, during the last centuries, helped to point out the alternatives facing mankind. The scope for political action is organized by and around models to which all of us make frequent reference and which constitute the pillars of both conservatism and reform. Even if the columns are somewhat fragile, the edifice is important: it has become part of our intellectual heritage, more so than we consciously recognize. All of us build our philosophy of society, past, present or future, by reference to these constructs. This is why it is highly *unrealistic* to minimize the importance of the end-products of normative theory, and why these models deserve to be considered more

closely, paying particular attention to the way in which they affect our thinking.

Even if we cannot describe or even list summarily here the various models which have ever been built, we need to examine some of the characteristics of these products, both in the minds of their authors and in terms of their effects on the 'recipients' – that is, all of us.[8] The best way to begin is to look at the characteristics of the most comprehensive models, those which purport to give a complete picture of the 'good society' and which at their extreme propose a utopian view of the world. We will then consider the more diffuse, but perhaps wider influence of selected parts, ideological concepts of these models, which help us daily to categorize men and their pronouncements in the field of politics.

A. *The good society and the utopias.* Normative theorists are not the only makers of utopias. Because of the links between the various schools of the discipline, other political scientists engage, at least in part, in utopia-building. Indeed, the making of utopias is subsumed unconsciously or consciously, directly or indirectly, in a wide variety of political-science analyses. Conversely, many normative theorists disclaim their involvement in 'utopia-making' on one of two grounds: critics in the strict sense, such as 'critical linguists', to whom we referred in the previous section, assert that they are concerned only with the internal logic of sets of concepts and of relations between concepts; and many normative thinkers, who view themselves as pragmatists, try to demonstrate that utopias are unrealistic and would rather be defined as 'utopia-unmakers' than as 'utopia-makers'.

We considered the case of linguists in the previous section: their linguistic analysis is of relevance merely because other thinkers, who are engaged in model-building, adapt these concepts to society and mankind. Individually, critical linguists may be justified in stating that they are not involved in the process of utopia-making; but their activities relate globally to those of others who are engaged in utopia-making, and they are therefore dependent on the existence of utopias. Pragmatists, on the other hand, appear both near to a mixed 'normative-

---

[8] A number of histories of political thought are quoted in the Bibliography.

descriptive' position and quite opposed to utopia-making;[9] their position seems, at first sight, to be closest to the truly half-way house position in which political thinkers 'should be'.

Of course, it can be logically held that to refuse to build uto-pias is itself a form of utopia-building. This is not sophistry; the argument parallels that by which normative political scientists criticize empiricists: in the end, there is a value-judgement, whether in the choice of subject-matter, or in the choice of indi-cators, or in both. Similarly, the normative theorist who opposes the building of utopias in principle does so because he rejects the idea that there might be some distant 'good society'; this surely amounts to saying that the society that exists is 'good', or that it is the best that can be found and/or organized (implying a pes-simistic view of human nature). But this standpoint is utopian. It satisfies all the requirements of a utopia – one of which is that the theorist should demonstrate that his view of the relative important of various principles entails the creation (or main-tenance) of one particular society. The anti-utopian may have an easy task, because he may simply state that 'order' is for him the most important value – and it would follow that the present society is necessarily better than any other since creating a new one would involve at least *some* disorder. Indeed, it would even follow that any present society, in any polity, is better than any other. But, since we know that one principle is never overriding in all circumstances, this position is untenable, at least in ex-treme cases. As principles have to be 'combined', and are not in a clear hierarchy, anti-utopians will be 'forced' to find other normative grounds for justifying existing society; they will have to demonstrate that the particular mix of values of an existing society is '*the* good one' or the best that can be achieved, a task as impossible as that which leads the utopian to discuss what man could be in another, unknown society.[10]

But whether based on logic or not, the debate *does* exist: many normative political theorists – particularly of the 'English school' – believe that the very idea of a good society, projected in

[9] See in particular the works of another representative of the English school of normative theory, which is primarily 'critical' in its approach: M. Oakeshott, and especially his *Rationalism in Politics* (Methuen, London, 1962).

[10] For a development of this point, see A. Arblaster and S. Lukes, eds., *The Good Society* (Methuen, London, 1971), pp. 6-11.

the future, is futile and dangerous. Much of their attitude stems probably from a deep-seated distrust of generalizations and extrapolations removed from reality. These normative theorists adopt positions which resemble those of empirical or descriptive political scientists: their argument is that there are so many unknowns that it is deluding readers to suggest that a utopia has a more than random chance of success.

So we find ourselves faced with the same dilemma as at the end of the previous section, regarding the nature of man. We naturally looked for a solution by linking criticisms and hopes in a precise and scientific basis for the utopia. This was at the root of Marx's efforts, though a similar trend can be distinguished in the early nineteenth century in such positivists as Comte or the Saint-Simonians. Marx remains crucial to this debate, however, because of his widespread influence in the past and present. He purported to develop a scientific theory and he sharply criticized those of his predecessors whom he labelled 'utopian' because their analyses were not based on an examination of real world history, however right or near-right he thought their principles were. Thus Marx can be placed half-way between pragmatists and strict utopians: his form of scientific utopianism attempted to reconcile the two approaches by showing that, contrary to what pragmatists thought, some utopias could be realized (indeed according to Marx would *necessarily* be realized), though the process had to follow a particular course. (And of course the blueprint for the future society was left very vague in Marx's own writings.)

The dilemma over utopias therefore reflects the basic predicament of political science. Given that, despite his major contributions to the analysis of society and politics, Marx did not succeed in ending the debate over utopias any more than any previous writers had done before him, his endeavour can only reinforce the opinion that utopias must remain the language of the dialogue between normative theorists. Marx's attempt epitomizes the role of constraints, which can neither be wholly rejected nor be wholly accepted; political scientists recognize – at least unconsciously – that the 'rules of the game' (the present society) can be changed in *some* circumstances; thus the creation of utopias paves the way to changing the rules by presenting possible systems governed by different rules – either based on different principles or on a different hierarchy of principles.

Both utopia-building and pragmatism play a major part in disseminating a 'culture' of social and political construction. Though this does not justify *any* construction which might be made by a would-be normative theorist, society as a whole gains markedly from the overall dialogue which these constructs provide.

B. *Ideologies.* Everyone who has political views and attitudes has, in a more or less inchoate form, an ideology: this is one area where interaction occurs between normative theory and empirical work, and it is probably the most developed and the most successful of these areas. An ideology is a set of interrlated attitudes which indicate a specific approach to society's problems. A conservative ideology, for instance, manifests itself in a number of ways, ranging from a 'repressive' attitude to crime through the desire to maintain unchallenged hierarchies in industry to an argument that education should not be given uniformly to the population as many would not truly benefit from the new opportunities which would be given to them. The word 'ideology' has become widely used, even quite outside the relatively refined sphere of political science and even professional politics. It is a means by which people can, so to speak, recognize each other politically, as soldiers know their comrades from their enemies by their uniforms.

When one starts analysing the implications of the concept of 'ideology', one runs into numerous problems, however. At the practical level, men do not hold consistent views to political questions as the idea of ideology implies; so one must look for the reasons for these inconsistencies, and probe deeper into the attitudes of men, a problem partly connected to questions of knowledge and interest in politics.[11] The difficulties become more serious at the theoretical level, as there may be doubts about the specific ideological 'compounds' which may be created. A repressive attitude towards crime belongs perhaps

---

[11] Much 'behavioural' analysis has indeed been devoted to showing how 'unideological' in terms of consistency men are, and how unhelpful they are in broad models. See for instance A. Campbell *et al., The American Voter* (Wiley, New York, 1960), Chapter 9, pp. 188-215; and S. M. Lipset, *Political Man* (Doubleday, New York, 1960), Chapters 4 and 5, pp. 97-176. This does not diminish the importance of the study of ideology.

naturally to conservatism, but can all types of permissive-ness be labelled 'radical'? Those who oppose smoking or heavy drinking in modern industrial societies do not consider themselves as 'conservative'. Equally serious difficulties are raised by the relationship between means and ends: it has been suggested that ideologies should be compared, not just by reference to *one* dimension (such as conservatism *v.* radicalism) but by reference to two, or perhaps several dimensions.[12] Neither the theory nor the empirical base are yet so satisfactory that political scientists consider ideologies an entirely satisfactory 'show-piece' of political-science results.

Yet, however imperfect it may be, the area of ideologies is of major importance because of its contribution to a general understanding of politics and to the prediction of the behaviour of others. Without such a concept, comprehension of the politics of others within society, and relationships between men would often become more difficult: there would be no easy recognition of each other's goals. This is why the concept was invented, and why it spread with the increasing participation of the population in politics. Alignments resulting from parties implied an alignment on the intellectual basis of the parties: ideologies provided this intellectual base. As long as the people were not at all, or were scarcely involved, problems of consistency or inconsistency were of little moment; with the advent of modern democracy this was all changed.

In this context ideologies are especially important because they link normative theories and real-world descriptions. But, though the concept of ideologies is accepted by all, there are similar debates about them between political thinkers as about utopias. All agree that *some* people have ideologies, but not all are agreed that everyone adheres to an ideology. But the pragmatist approach to ideologies can be refuted in the same way as the pragmatist approach to utopias: to refuse to recognize one's ideology is a form of ideology. Just as pragmatists prefer conservative utopias (the present society is good, or the best which can be achieved), they also prefer conservative ideologies; they refuse to consider themselves imprisoned in the straightjacket of

[12] See H. J. Eysenck, *The psychology of politics* (Routledge and Kegan Paul, London, 1954), Chapter 6, 'Ideology and Temperament', in particular pp. 177 and ff.

a general philosophy because they rate current arrangements to
be acceptable and to need only minor adjustments.

Behind this opposition lies the further cleavage between those
who do and those who do not believe in a systematic approach to
social and political change. Ideological constructs are
classificatory schemes, or even typologies: they show that the
same methodology is shared in the various branches of political
science, by normative theorists as well as by those who are primarily concerned with describing facts. So they are liable to
those criticisms made against classificatory systems in general.
Reality may not conform to the classification, both because
individuals often do not have 'consistent' ideologies and because it is theoretically difficult to group all types of policy in an
ideological scheme. But the pragmatists' recipe of taking a
piecemeal view suffers from the flaw of substituting no understanding for partial understanding. Though ideological analysis is clumsy, its power emphasizes the value – empirical and
practical, as well as theoretical – of the normative approaches to
political problems.

The end-products of normative theory span a wide range of
levels – from the most 'impractical' utopias to the recognition of
the ideologies that men adopt when they choose particular
policies. Normative political theory is neither a rather 'amusing'
but somewhat superfluous superstructure of political analysis,
nor the only hope for guiding mankind towards a better society.
It is not the former because it is constantly brought back to
practical life, perhaps despite the wishes of normative political
theorists, who would prefer it to be highly theoretical all the
time. It is not the latter precisely because of this need for a realistic basis and because of the difficulties involved in any projected society for mankind. There are too many loopholes in normative analysis which cannot be sewn up. Normative theorists
themselves are divided, both by their ideologies and by their
type of intellectual approach to the problem of the good society:
those who are less sanguine about the future development of the
analysis act as a permanent brake on those who are perhaps too
eager to engage in building wider and more imaginative constructs which are too often unrealistic.

Normative political theory makes a major contribution to

society by clarifying its aims, and is therefore an important part of the discipline of political science. The very debate which normative theorists conduct among themselves, part of which permeates to the broader public, on liberty *v.* equality, on tradition *v.* reform, on authority *v.* permissiveness, for instance, contributes to the political education of that public and is an integral part of the general contribution of normative theory to our knowledge of politics. But normative theory must constantly refer to reality; in this way it shares the common predicament of all aspects of political science: one branch of the discipline refers and relates to the others. To understand the possible impact of normative theory, we need therefore to turn to another branch, that of the description of happenings, and examine the problems which political thinkers face in analysing behaviour.

CHAPTER 6

Behavioural Theory

Political scientists have often been inclined to reserve the title of 'theory' to normative inquiries, while the analysis of politics 'as it is' is viewed as descriptive rather than theoretical. But this view is undermined at present, partly because it has been recognized that the 'great works' of the 'classical theorists' include much description, and partly because behavioural or analytical theory has markedly developed and become an important branch of political analysis. Early behavioural studies were very specific – they were concerned with actions of prime ministers or cabinets, with the rise of party leaders, with the 'anatomy' of 'great events'; but, more and more, analyses have become systematic and emphasize general trends: works on Stalin, for example, discuss the means which dictators have to use to fulfil their aims; works on prime ministers and cabinets discuss the extent to which decisions are individual or collective. As general lessons are drawn, we move from description to theory.

But behavioural theory has gone further: it has begun to embark on general studies of the political process. Under the influence of economists, analytical political theorists have attempted to discover principles and laws accounting for political developments in every type of situation and in every form of environment.

This effort has hitherto been only partly successful. First, the tension between the conflicting demands of detailed descriptions and general conclusions has not been overcome: the immense variety of political situations is a problem. It may be an attractive goal to look for general laws of political behaviour explaining how men react in all circumstances; but the context plays an important part in the making of a decision, and every political event has unique features. Second, context often means institutions, procedures, laws and constitutions – what we called the structural part of political life. If general laws of politics are to be devised, they have to apply equally to an absolute regime such as Saudi Arabia, a large liberal democracy such as the United States and a closed and yet dynamic modern State such as the Soviet Union. It may be that the President of the United States 'plays' politics with congressional leaders and that the Secretary General of the Communist Party of the Soviet Union also 'plays' politics with the members of the Politburo of that Party and with other Soviet Leaders; but the structures in each case are so different that it is necessary at least to understand them. So we can see the need to study both general arrangements and the specific interaction between politicians; this goes back to the distinction which we drew in Chapter 3 between mico- and macro-politics.

Of course, it may be suggested that the study of political behaviour in general will help at a later stage to bring the study of structures closer to the study of behaviour. In the natural sciences, it has been possible – at least to some extent – to look for the small particles or elements behind the larger objects seen by the naked eye. But this has taken time; given the complexity of both structures and of behaviour in political life, even the study of behaviour on a general and 'systematic' basis remains hazardous: the examination of the precise link between structures and behaviour will have to be left to future generations.

I.   *The common elements of political life*
Historians have long attempted to 'explain' political events; so, in a way, they have been students of political behaviour. But historians do not normally ask themselves what is common to all political life: they emphasize distinctions and concentrate on the variety of situations.

Yet even historians cannot be entirely guided by the flow of events which they are studying: if they are to explain, they must discover patterns, though they may be reluctant to recognize the importance of these patterns. But by using general expressions which help to classify and identify some modes of behaviour, they are already moving in the direction of behavioural theory. 'Dictators dominate their followers.' 'Popular leaders influence others:' these are general criteria which form the beginnings of an analytical theory of politics.

The difference between a political historian who studies an event and a behavioural theorist who wishes to discover laws of political activity is thus a matter of degree and of conscious recognition of the need to define the basic elements of political life. While the historian may never have to be concerned with a definition of these elements, a general analysis of political activity has to look for the 'bare bones', so to speak, of political events. A prime minister is appointed; a law is passed by Parliament: these are different events which entail the involvement of many different persons in many different ways. Yet, in both these events, there are similarities: some have put pressure on others and have been successful; and the means of pressure may have been similar in both situations. The point is not to deny that there are differences, but to stress that similarities have also to be studied so that there can be a better understanding of these and other events.

Indeed, we do not need to look very far to find the similarities in every political event. First, every political happening takes the form of a *chain* of related decisions. The chain can be so long that we might not succeed in finding all the elements nor be exactly sure where it began. But at least in theory we could subdivide the whole operation into a very large, perhaps, but still finite, number of elements. Every political event is thus the summary of a set of *decisions*.

These decisions all have one common characteristic. If we view the chain of events as being self-contained, we can immediately see an important dimension that needs to be examined – the dimension of *time*. Laws need time to be adopted; decisions of leaders always take some time to be elaborated. A number of 'causes' – the pressure of groups and of individuals, physical accidents, personal thinking – come into play over this period. The way they relate to each other in this period leads to the final decision.

Time is the operating factor; the decision is the end-product; but the action or actions which take place are produced by people. No political event 'happens' in a purely physical sense: politics implies the action of people. The starting point may be a physical event, for instance an earthquake, but the matter becomes political only when *someone* suggests that 'Something must be done about it.' Though it may be useful, or simpler, to concentrate on cases where the chain of events started with a physical happening, we still at some point have to identify the actions of the men who came to be involved. In all political life, we shall have to look at *actors* coming to a *decision* after a period of *time*.

A. *Actors*. A decision will be explained if we can state the reasons why some people took a particular stand at a given moment of time and if we can demonstrate that the combination of actions and reactions had to produce that outcome. This is, indeed, a tall order, and we may have to be satisfied with relatively weak approximations of a full explanation.

To begin with, we have to be able to identify the 'actors'. This may seem very simple: we talk of prime ministers, cabinets and leaders of political parties as 'taking decisions'; but these individuals or groups of individuals do not (at least normally) operate in a vacuum. The prime minister is constantly subjected to influences or pressures of various kinds: when he takes the decision to dissolve Parliament, for instance, what other individuals or groups of individuals can be said to have been influential, directly or indirectly, in convincing the prime minister? No one can ever know for sure. But how can we begin to approach the problem?

The difficulty centres round the determination of the universe of actors whom we shall deem to have been at least in part instrumental in the decision process. We need to have some guidelines which will enable us to include some persons and to exclude others. But any guidelines which we might have are very imprecise. We might try to use proximity: for example, someone who sees another drowning will jump to his rescue simply because he is nearby; those who worry about a town's housing, educational, or other services, are likely to be those who live in the town. But proximity is clearly insufficient: intellectual proximity seems often as important as physical nearness. We then might consider the ties by which men are linked: family, ethnic or religious ties; occupational or class ties. There may be also legal ties: for example, membership of committees is determined by rules. So, in defining the universe of actors, students of political behaviour are obliged to take into account broad factors influencing inclusion and exclusion: these factors, more often than not, are precisely the structures – institutions, procedures, social groups – which pattern and organize the broadest relationships in the society.

But to decide who the actors are is not enough. We have also to be able to say why the various actors came to a given decision. At this point we may be tempted to avoid the issue and claim that the decision was 'inevitable': for instance, we may say that the rate of inflation was such that the government 'had' to tighten credit. But the government could have tightened it more or less, it could have allowed for some exceptions and not others, it could even have resigned rather than tighten credit. If we then recognize that at least *some* of the result could have been different – if we do not accept that *all*, strictly all, of the decision was due, for instance, to economic forces – we are then confronted with what might be described as a 'psychological assumption', namely that the efforts of some have an effect on actions of others.

No one has ever denied the 'psychological assumption'. Although Marxists claim that economic forces are the political substructure and social and political events a mere superstructure, they still leave at least some leeway, in practice, for the role of individual action. There is no full and complete 'reductionism' which could entirely explain interpersonal reactions in terms of habits, religious fear or economic forces. But while leaving scope for individuals and apparently restoring some individual freedom in interpersonal actions, this also poses serious problems to the behavioural theorist as he has to explain the particular sequence that leads one individual to 'follow' another, to be 'influenced' by a third, or to 'dominate' a fourth.

To say that actors have some part to play in the determination of decisions is therefore also to state the need for a theory of interpersonal relations. If those who think politically could account for the whole of politics by relating every individual action to broader forces, they would, in the end, deny the existence of politics; but since they, more realistically, recognize that there is some potential for individual action, they have to enter the complex labyrinth of interpersonal influence, counter-influence, pressure and counter-pressure.

B. *Time*. Before we examine the efforts which have to be made to account for the ways in which actors interact, we must explore the characteristics of time and of decisions. Time is the dimension along which politics takes place; it is also a very helpful element, since it enables us to order events sequentially: A acts in a certain way at a given moment; B then reacts at a subsequent period. The threads may occasionally – indeed often – be interwoven: after all, B may only find much later what A did do, and he may have already reacted on the mistaken impression that A would act differently. But this is only a complication of a 'practical' kind; it does not affect the principle of the investigation.

What does affect the investigation more profoundly is the recognition that time has very 'different values', so to speak, for different individuals. Some men act more quickly than others; there are slow thinkers and slow decision-makers, as well as quick thinkers and decision-makers. For some, 'Time is money'; for others, time is unimportant – or seems to be. There seems to be no common denominator: the importance of the decision is clearly not the only yardstick which we can use to measure the 'rate' of decision-making.

Time has thus a 'subjective', more than a truly interpersonal character. But time in politics is also composed of distinct elements. We may talk of the 'political process', the 'electoral process', or the 'bargaining process', but these are short-cut expressions. In reality, behind these processes, we find a series of 'stops and starts'. One day, someone will take a decision; then, one, two or three days later, someone else will react. The government decides on a policy; opponents take some time to organize: they may then announce a meeting or a demonstration; later, the government will react. There are discontinuities, rather than a process.

Because of these discontinuities, those who think politically are likely to enter a discussion of time with the utmost caution. As the number of actors grows, and as the time span increases, the sporadic and heterogeneous character of time also becomes more marked. Consequently, it is usually impossible to chart the progress of an event. It is in particular very hard to isolate the various elements of these discontinuities and measure their effect. Efforts have been made from time to time to attempt to measure the extent of violence in a given country,[1] the assumption being that if one were able to measure the rate of the spread of violence, one would be able to make predictions about the future of a country in the way one can make predictions about the future of a currency by reference to the progress of the balance of payments. But there are too many interruptions, even considering those incidents of violence which are relatively homogeneous for a given country. If we try to take into account the possible effects of a variety of activities of numerous actors over time variations become such that any measurement against time is truly impossible.

So one is tempted to solve the difficulty by remaining at a level where discontinuities are least: to study decisions at a micro level, thus avoiding the distortions and variations arising from different institutional frames of reference. Yet, even here, there is a problem raised by the differing rates of reaction. Actions are the result of a process of becoming involved in politics: the best that can be said is that the process 'takes time', but a time that is so individualized and so idiosyncratic that it ceases to provide a common element for the analysis.

C. *Decisions.* Assuming that we have identified the actors and at least noted their actions and reactions over time, the problem of what constitutes a decision remains. Up to now, we have taken it for granted that we knew what a decision was: it *followed* the set of actions and reactions over time that we have identified and linked. Yet a number of problems arise.

First, it is true that a decision implies that from a formal point of view, something has been accepted as a policy by the community. But this is to concentrate on the results – on what will (supposedly) happen after the decision has been taken. If we are concerned with the sequence of events which produces the decision, we have to relate the decision to what happened *before* it took place. Strictly, there is no way of explaining the decision from the previous set of actions, as a decision is of a different order: here we come up against another discontinuity. A process of actions and reactions (which might have gone on indefinitely) is broken by the intervention of some *deus ex machina* which seems to suggest that a crucial point has arrived. Various people

See for instance T. R. Gurr, *Why men rebel* (Princeton U.P., Princeton, 1970).

discuss and debate: at some point they stop – and decide. A
leader thinks about a problem: he then stops and decides. There
are two ways of explaining why a decision is taken at a given
moment of time: one is, again, through structures: 'on a certain
day, there will be a vote on the matter'; the other is a psychological explanation: through the increased tension arising from
actions and reactions, one individual or set of individuals
'cracks' and 'gives in'. In both cases we have had to introduce an
element distinct from the set of actions and reactions over time.

Second, the part played by the decision in the analysis is that
of a prize in a competition. It implies the success of those who
had championed this particular formula. Decisions are not only
important because they are the stuff of politics – which is why
political thinkers have to go back to analyse the chain of events
which preceded them – they are also important yardsticks. They
are the technical tools by which political thinkers measure the
possible actions and reactions of individuals. If we want to assess
whether an individual was strong or weak, we look at his decisions and assess his ability to affect the community of which he
was, in whatever capacity, a leader. But in order to do this, we
have to be able to assess what would have happened had the
individual not been able to effect events in the way he did, because this is the only way of measuring the discrepancy between
what did happen and what could have happened. It is no use
measuring (or attempting to assess by whatever means) the
strength of an individual or of a group of individuals in the
abstract: one has to refer to what might 'realistically' have happened. But logically it is nonsense to talk about what might
realistically have happened. If the decision did take place, no
other decision could realistically have happened, since it did not
happen!

One is sometimes able to avoid the difficulty by drawing
comparisons between similar circumstances to see whether the
same decisions have indeed been taken. Various prime ministers
may propose similar policies but only some may be followed or
be successful. Of course comparisons raise serious problems: the
conditions have to be identical for conclusions to be drawn. And
it seems necessary to examine a large number of decisions if one
is to draw conclusions which will be recognized as generally
valid: but the more decisions one comes to consider, the more

difficult it becomes to find conditions which are identical.

Third, it is never truly the case that one can isolate a decision and study its actors independently from other decisions in the overall chain. Every decision seems to dissolve into smaller elements each of which can be considered as being a decision in need of special study. The decision of a cabinet is preceded by decisions of sub-groups; the appointment of a leader is preceded by previous appointments to various positions of members of the body who make the appointment.

As political scientists face these problems when they wish to describe an event or analyse the elements of political life, they try to avoid hasty and oversimplified generalizations. Yet we must remember that we are trying to analyse political behaviour in the context of political events. Some general analysis of decision-making has therefore to be devised: however unsatisfactory the current state of analytical theory may be and however difficult it may be to describe precisely decisions, time and actors, it is not possible to avoid efforts towards generalizations.

II.   *The analysis of decisions*

We are therefore obliged to accept that political events are a series of decisions taken by actors in a given period. If we are to look for explanations of a general character, we have to concentrate on the relationships between the various actors and see how these relationships may lead over time to some final product which will be recognized as the decision taken by the various actors who have come together. This of course seems simple: we are not particularly concerned when we hear daily that a given body has 'made a decision'. Yet there is much mystery in these procedures. If people were agreed about a common course, we could easily see why they also agreed to take a decision; but we cannot slide over the problems that are commonly raised by disagreements. X, we say, was 'defeated', for instance, in his bid for party leadership: but why did he 'give in'? It is not always the case that he was *actually* compelled to withdraw or get out. The 'majority' decided, we may say: but is the majority always accepted by all as being *the* one means of forcing individuals to accept decisions? Politics is in fact *rarely* achieved through strict majority: pressures of various kinds, insidious or overt, are common methods of coming to decisions.

We have therefore to examine more closely the types of relationships which lead to changes in the positions taken by the various actors. Actors come to the discussion table with an attitude; in various circumstances, they change these views. Those who think politically cannot afford to gloss over these problems: there are too many differences, too many subtle distinctions between forms of pressure and forms of influence that we have to clarify the types of human relationships through which they work.

A. *Types of human relationships in the decision process.* A free vote is to take place in Parliament on an issue; speeches are made by various M.P.s for and against the proposal; some members change their position 'as a result' of these speeches. This is, on the surface, a simple – and common – happening; yet what happens in the minds of the M.P.s is not very clear. We may say that 'argument' has convinced these M.P.s, but why does argument convince some M.P.s but not all? In order to explain why the various M.P.s divided in the end in a given manner, we obviously must probe deeply into motivations. One man may be convinced because one of his friends spoke in a certain way; another may be convinced because some constituents happened to talk to him while the debate was on; a third may have realized consequences which he had not foreseen.

Yet this is only one of the types of situations in which actors come to move from their early positions. When the situation is tense, threats of various kinds may have the effect of 'forcing' individuals to change their positions. A prime minister may have to call in his supporters and point out that their careers may be seriously impaired if they continue to behave in a certain fashion; dictators may simply have their police round up those who might be opposed to their authority.

These are some of the types of general explanations which are usually given for the moves made by some actors. It seems that there are means by which it is possible to make others do what they would not have done if these means were not used; but it also seems that these means vary greatly. Not surprisingly, anyone who is concerned with an analysis of political behaviour will be trying to put some order into what seems, at first sight, a very complex jig-saw.

B. *Power* v. *exchange*. Stalin forced an agricultural revolution on an obviously unwilling peasantry; military leaders oblige a government to resign; the mayor of a town convinces his council to provide land for new industries: these are all ways in which a decision is made 'against' the desires of others. Though the process of the decision-making is different, one element seems to be common: those who win seem to have displayed *power* over those who lose. And as the analysis of political behaviour is concerned with decisions taken over time by some actors, the analysis of power seems to be one of the major keys to the understanding of political behaviour. Not surprisingly, many behavioural theorists have been concentrated on such an analysis – and some have even gone as far as suggesting that the whole of political activity could be viewed in terms of power.

Power seems to be particularly useful because it appears to encompass a variety of types of 'successful political pressure': it covers gentler forms of inducement, often described as influence; it covers much stronger forms of domination; and it covers legal and illegal forms of control: a political leader may or may not have had the 'authority' to act, but he may still have been able to force his followers to comply.

Indeed, power seems to be more than a general way of describing the 'superiority' of some over others; it appears also able to monitor subtle differences between individuals, rather than merely help to distinguish between broad categories. It seems to provide a comparative scale of evaluation at all levels and in all situations.[2] It is as good over time as it is for the instant: the power of an individual may increase or decrease; the power relationship between two people may be reversed.

There is a limit, however: despite the generality of the concept, power cannot be extended to cover group relationships. We may say that Stalin had power over the Russians, that the British Prime Minister has power over his colleagues, or that a strong mayor has power over town councillors. But we cannot use the word with the same meaning if we talk of the 'power' of trade unions over a party or in a nation, or of the secret police over various organizations. We are no longer considering relationships between individuals. We are considering institutions

[2] See in particular R. A. Dahl, 'The concept of power', *Behavioral Science* 2 (July 1957), pp. 201-15.

and other arrangements within a society. Nor do we give power the same meaning when we compare the power of two individuals and when we take into account institutions, procedures, social forces; in trying to assess the relationships between actors, it is very difficult to limit the inquiry to that relationship and ignore factors such as influence, domination, authority and other forms of control.

There is a more serious difficulty, however. Even if we were to view all relationships by which an individual eventually pushes another to act in a given way as manifestations of power, there are many important occasions in politics when no actor gives in, and a compromise is achieved. A may be influenced or threatened by B; we may say that B has power. But perhaps A realizes that if he does what B wants, he will be able to extract from B some advantage at a later point in time; indeed A may suggest to B some form of arrangement which might equally suit A and B. Typically, we view these relationships as relationships of equality, not exercises of power. And situations of this type seem to occur frequently, for instance in committees, or between various governments. It is difficult to say whether equality is or is not more common than inequality in political relationships: but it is clear that both types of situations occur.

We seem then to have complicated seriously our conceptual analysis: we seem to have not one, but at least two, bases on which to look for relationships. Those who analyse political behaviour naturally oscillate between the two approaches. Like normative theorists looking for an overriding principle, some behaviourists have attempted to give precedence to power, while others have emphasized bargaining; and, like normative theorists in their search for this principle, they have typically failed. For instance, it is true that often what looks like a command is, to some extent, based on bargaining: the prime minister may be able to induce some followers to toe the party line, but he may have to placate them, perhaps by giving them a job. But can one really reduce all political activity to such a relationship? What does the frightened citizen get out of obeying a dictator? One might say that he gets relief from fear; one might also say that the dictator has to take into account the reactions of his subjects to make sure that he does not go too far, and that this, too, is a form of bargain. But this is overstretching the notion. Trade-offs occur where there is near-equality between the various actors; when there is gross inequality, there *is* influence, domination, and various other forms of power. It seems impossible to limit the analysis of relationships between actors to one concept.

C. *The question of measurement.* The analysis of power and of bargaining cannot stop at the discovery of concepts. If these concepts are to be useful in political analysis, they have to enable behavioural theorists to compare adequately the various situations which they wish to study, and some form of measurement will need to be undertaken.

In principle, as we saw, power is a versatile and incremental concept: we can conceive of subtle distinctions between individuals, but, in practice, the measurement is most problematic. The political scientist who wishes to measure power is in a much less fortunate position than the economist who wishes to measure wealth. The economist has at his disposal numbers which indicate values; the political scientist finds it very difficult to say that an individual has a number of 'units' of power. He can try various indirect means of measuring power by means of comparisons: for instance, comparing pairs of individuals in relation to the same problem. He may also use subjective assessments, and ask panels of 'judges' to compare the power of various men. But none of these techniques is really satisfactory; as we said in Chapter 2, the best that can be achieved is a system of contrived values over which there will be little agreement even between the experts, let alone throughout the public.

The only solution would be to avoid numbers altogether. Unfortunately, for the time being at least, techniques of measurement without numbers are still underdeveloped. Theoretically, one could imagine that the power of various individuals could be assessed by the discovery of changes in patterns of relationships and by the comparison of these patterns. In a decision-making process, the moves of various individuals correspond to as many changes in patterns of relationship over time; if these changes are very large, the patterns of relationships will be markedly altered; if changes are small, the patterns will tend to be the same. As new forms of mathematics, such as topological analysis, develop amd become increasingly successful at comparing different patterns of relationships, it might be possible to trace precisely the differences in power between individuals.[3] It is much too early to know whether such techniques will eventually produce real results, but they have more potential than repeated efforts to give numbers to 'quantities' of power which do not correspond to any generally accepted numbers in the minds of non-specialists.

The measurement of power is thus fraught with difficulties; but the analysis of bargaining and exchange has progressed more rapidly with the help of the technique of game theory. Exchange in political life is often based on confrontations between two or more individuals wishing to obtain the best possible result for all of them. The effort is therefore to try to maximize the advantages, not just for one individual, but for all. Game theory provides at least some mathematical tools to handle these situations. But the technique is still insufficiently developed to help resolve many important problems of bargaining. It has had practical uses in some aspects of international relations: it is often said that the United States and the Soviet Union have acted on the basis of the results of 'simulated' situations which have been 'played' in advance by State and Defence Department officials. It also had educational value in helping to demonstrate to those who are not engaged in politics the nature of the tensions and crises which occur in leaders' confrontations.[4] But it is not able to handle situations where the number of players is large: it is in fact most useful where only two players are involved. And it is entirely based on some common agreement about the best possible solution that the players should achieve.

When, on the contrary, actors do not agree on the *value* of goals, game theory is of little use. In an ordinary game, players want to win: they agree on that overall goal. In economics, players agree about the overall aim: each wants to obtain the greatest possible monetary advantage. But, in politics, goals are

[3] Most of the formal analysis of political science does take place within the context of more classical mathematics, admittedly, but there is a perceptible tendency to use topology both in sociology and political science.

[4] See H. A. Alker, *Mathematics and Politics* (Macmillan, London, 1965), pp. 130-146, for an appreciation of the role of game theory in political science.

many and varied: it is often not the case that they all want to achieve the same object, because their views about what is the best can markedly differ. In international relations, it is generally assumed (and this is seemingly realistic *now*, at least as regards world wars) that the players (the governments) want to maximize the chances of peace; but this was not the case before 1945; and it is not the case with respect to 'limited' wars. In other aspects of politics, what the actors want to win is often quite unclear: some want to achieve a particular policy, others want to gain prestige; some may give priority to a problem that others may consider to be utterly trivial.

D. *The study of communication.* The concepts of power and bargaining refer to relationships between relatively few actors; it is in practice difficult to analyse precisely, let alone to measure, the power a world leader exercises over millions of followers; and bargaining between large numbers of individuals has not been studied, nor even been clearly defined. But another fundamental relationship relates dynamically, not only small groups of actors, but the less involved mass of the public: the communication link.

Indeed, communication is the basis of all human relationships: power and bargaining cannot occur without communication. The strength of the most ruthless dictator stops at the point where he no longer communicates with his followers and with the citizens of the country which he rules. Many authoritarian leaders did lose control because they had become the prisoners of a few advisers – and ceased to communicate with the broad mass. If a dictator is unaware of feelings and movements at the grass roots, his actions may be seriously misjudged. Similarly, an army faced with a wall of silence from an occupied population can often do no more than guard its own outposts.

The concept of communication has therefore attracted the attention of political scientists as being perhaps the best tool and the most general means at their disposal. Indeed, a general theory of communication might seem able in the long run to describe the role of structures: an institution is, to a very large extent, characterized by 'privileged' relationships; it establishes links between some individuals and not others: it creates 'borders' which stop communication flowing from one side to the other. This can easily be shown empirically: there is more communication between the citizens of one nation than across national boundaries, as a count of correspondence exchanged between private citizens would show.[5]

Yet a study of communication is also hampered by problems of measurement which have not yet been overcome. It is relatively simple to measure the flow of public and semi-public communication between individuals, be they private citizens or public officials and politicians; but public communication reveals only a fraction of the exchanges that take place in any community. The flow of ideas takes place to a very large extent through private forms of communication, in informal meetings where two, three or a few individuals discuss casually, but frequently, the problems which they face. And these private exchanges often seem more important than public forms of communication; they do appear to shape the ideology of individuals more profoundly, probably because they are more repeated and more frank.

Moreover, even if communication could be measured adequately, it would not provide an explanatory model of developments within society. The theory of bargaining is based on the broad principle that individuals exchange the 'goods' (in the broadest sense) that they wish to obtain: it seems reasonable to assume that men want to 'maximize' their 'happiness' at least to the extent that they are able to perceive what goods will satisfy them most. The concept of power – and the associated concepts of influence, domination, authority, etc. – seems to correspond to our common experience of inequality among individuals. Some men can achieve more than others, whether because of their physical or intellectual advantages or because they are better able to use to their benefit the chances that society may give them.

But communication does not help to explain relationships in a similar fashion. It only registers a succession of events and enables us to notice that there are gaps in the fabric of human relationships. It circumscribes the area in which bargaining will

[5] This type of analysis was first conducted empirically on a comparative basis by K. W. Deutsch in *Nationalism and Social Communication* (M.I.T. Press, Chicago, 1953). This author then generalized his findings and developed a model of the role of communication in political life in *The Nerves of Government* (Free Press, New York, 1963).

take place and power will be exercised, to be sure; but it does not tell us *why* relationships exist between some men and not between others. While communication may therefore help to determine more precisely the consequences of the existence of institutions, procedures, and other arrangements, the reasons for the existence of these structures have to be found elsewhere. The study of communication is therefore likely to remain a study of the various ways in which men interact, not a study of the conditions of this interaction.

III.   *The end-products of behavioural theory: rational-choice models and beyond?*

Despite these difficulties, efforts at building a theory have been patient, numerous and important, in particular since the 1950s. Far from concluding that political studies should be confined to the description of individual cases, political scientists have endeavoured to discover general patterns of relationships by using increasingly formal techniques of analysis. The first wave of formal analysis has been mainly concerned with the study of bargaining largely because bargaining is so similar to the sort of interaction that takes place in economics, and therefore economic techniques could be applied. Economics is based on a theory of 'rational choice' according to which individuals attempt to maximize their own advantage by obtaining for themselves the largest possible share of the goods which they desire; so bargaining theory in politics has tended to be based on the same theory of rational choice. But this approach seemed too narrow; it appeared to cover only part – perhaps only a limited part – of political relations, either because bargains are not based on rational calculations or because, as we know, power and associated forms of pressure are an essential part of political activity. Hence a second wave of efforts, which have been devoted to an expansion of formal and general analysis beyond rational choice. The potential importance of these studies for the future of political analysis goes beyond the relatively limited results which have been achieved up to now.

   A. *'Rational-choice' models.* The theory of political behaviour has been influenced by economics: this is natural, since economics is the only social science which successfully developed formal models to a high degree of theoretical sophistication.

There are great similarities between the two fields: politics, as economics, is concerned with decisions, albeit decisions of a much broader and less readily measurable kind. It would be no exaggeration to say that economics is a special case of politics, the sphere of economics comprising the activities that are based on the monetary system; the sphere of politics comprising the activities that relate to any kind of collective decision in a community. Thus, naturally, many political decisions and processes of decision-making resemble economic decisions and processes of decision-making, in particular if there is a near-monetary aim or if the calculations of the actors before the decision are similar to the calculations of economic actors. In these areas, behavioural theory has successfully extended the ideas of economic theory, while at times encountering difficult problems of measurement, mainly in the area of bargaining, where the analysis led to the development of models usually collected under the label of 'rational-choice' models.[6]

We cannot enter here the controversy on the meaning of rationality: in politics, as elsewhere, the notion tends to elude analysis. Broadly, behaviour is said to be rational when it corresponds to a calculation of the best means of achieving chosen ends. The difficulty is that all activities can be described as rational if one takes into consideration, besides monetary gains, various other advantages such as psychological satisfaction. Thus one needs to narrow down the scope of the concept – something which is feasible in economics because monetary gains and losses determine the field, but is not as easy, indeed remains always arbitrary, in politics, because a variety of psychological gains (for example, career, idealistic drive) must be taken into account. One way of doing so is to restrict the analysis to the short-term, in fact to go to the opposite extreme from the analysis of the good society which we examined in the previous chapter. There cannot be a rational-choice model of 'absolute liberty' or of the 'civilization of plenty': these are so distant that means and ends become hazy and everything becomes contingent on the idiosyncrasies (beliefs) of the theorist. It is just not

[6] Perhaps the best-known and most influential examples of the use of a 'rational-choice' model has been that of A. Downs, *An Economic Theory of Democracy* (Harper & Row, New York, 1957), in which the author examines the way electors and parties 'will' behave under conditions of rationality.

possible to produce a model in the strict sense that economists might give to it; nor is it possible to see how one could develop an analysis of the process of bargaining or even of psychological influences which could advance the discussion.

Naturally, many rational-choice models have been even simpler and been concerned either with two-man situations or two-unit situations (as with two countries in an arms race, unions and employers in a conflict); in such situations, through the use of game theory in particular, it has been possible to state precisely what the optimum decision should be in relation to the clearly known goals of the two partners. Such models have produced significant results: for example, they contributed to the developments in disarmament in the 1960s and 1970s.[7] Similarly, rational-choice models can help to state clearly the different objectives which need to be optimized when a committee is confronted with a decision. One should not underestimate the extent to which decisions are normally taken in the dark, not because there is no *desire* to pursue any long-term ends, nor because there is ideological disagreement but because actors are often unclear about the objectives and the ways to reconcile them. Electoral processes in committees, for instance, can be particularly unrewarding – and paradoxical in their results.[8] Decisions can be proved to depend on the order in which the questions are put to the committee, unless variations in coalitions lead to insoluble and 'cyclical' negative majorities.[9]

A number of problems have been identified – and many of them solved – through the analysis of committee decision-making. But rational-choice models do not apply only to committee behaviour. They have been used, with some success, in other situations where large numbers are involved – in particular in the field of voting. If parties are considered as firms selling

[7] See in particular L. F. Richardson, *Arms and Insecurity* (Stevens, London, 1960).

[8] See D. Black, *The theory of Committees and Elections* (Cambridge University Press, London, 1958), in particular Chapters 12-16.

[9] See K. Arrow, *Social choice and individual values* (Wiley, London, 1951). For a further discussion and an important restriction on the role of these paradoxes in politics, see G. Tullock, *Toward a Mathematics of Politics* (University of Michigan Press, Michigan, 1967), Chapter 3, pp. 37-49.

products and competing in a market, one can determine the
rules which will help electors to draw the largest benefits as well
as the rules that will lead parties to gain majorities. Even if it is
true that neither parties nor electors are governed exclusively by
rational considerations of benefits to be gained, it is important
at least to know what consequences would ensue if a rational
mode of behaviour was adopted in a political system.[10] We can
then discover precisely the difference between reality and
rational behaviour.

Moreover, rational-choice models have also helped to
increase rigour in the discussion of political problems and in
particular in the study of means designed to achieve pre-
determined goals. One can deduce what consequences would
follow if a party were to adopt a given policy, first in terms of
support for the party in the country, second in terms of social
and economic achievements, and third in terms of the effect of
these achievements on long-term party support; then one can
begin to approximate a 'scientific analysis' of politics which is
radically different and appreciably more powerful than the
'hunches' on which many decisions are currently taken and
which are none the less typically followed despite the serious
consequences of many decisions for future generations.

B. *Beyond rational choice?* This is why it is idle to detail models
which are only beginning to be developed and which will be
improved as the analysis proceeds and as the limitations of previous models become more apparent. But much effort is devoted
precisely to devising models that go beyond the limitations of
rational choice and aim at a truly general descriptive theory. In
order to do so, three types of difficulties have to be solved: they
concern the collective character of the choices to be made in
politics, the motivations of the actors (and of potential actors)
and the overall constraints which political life, at given points of
time and space, imposes on actors. Though the first and second
of these problems can be met, it is difficult as yet to see how the
third can be dealt with.

We noted earlier that the methodology and successes of economists had attracted some political scientists to a more formal
analysis (and indeed some economists have been very instrumental in this development, by applying some of their skills and

[10] See A. Downs, *op. cit.*

methodology to political problems).[11] But, while analogies may be drawn in terms of a philosophy of bargaining which prevails in some types of decision-making, a major difference stems from the collective nature of the choices which have to be made. The successes of rational-choice models have occurred previously where there are only two actors (or two units, such as two countries, or an employer and a union): in such cases the 'collective choice' amounts to a choice which is acceptable to *each of two,* this is to say that the decision is applicable only to those who have participated in the bargain – a compromise at some point near the half-way mark may well be a good solution (though not always the optimal one). When the number of actors is very small – but greater than two – one may find the same compromise mid-way between the actors' interests. But most political decisions are *collective* in character, that is to say, they are applicable to a whole community which is very much larger than the numbers of persons who participated in the bargain; they are also often non-incremental, or are concerned with widely disparate choices, such as civil rights *v.* a higher standard of living. In practice, however, it has been possible, by a painful effort of measurement of attitudes, to go somewhat beyond the 'two-men' or 'small-group' situation. Preferences can be measured, albeit not very precisely. One can at least conceive of means of determining somewhat more precisely the relationship between these preferences. One could thus build complex models of collective choice. One can therefore imagine that one could go beyond two- or three-men situations and expand the range of problems which would be compared.

The second problem, that of motivation, is more difficult to circumvent. When considering motivations, we are moving some distance from the idea of rational choice, because of the complexities of the relationship between attitude and behaviour; between 'ideal motivations' and 'real' or 'instant' feelings about a problem. Is it rational to vote for a party which includes in its programme provisions which are likely to make one less well-off materially? Is it rational for the rich always to vote for right-wing parties? It may be in their long-term interests to see that the poorer classes are less poor, and therefore less prone to

[11] For instance K. Arrow, K. Boulding, A. Downs and E. Lindblom, to cite only a few American examples.

revolution: this is why rational-choice models tend to concentrate on the short-term. But there is more: some rich people may vote for a left-wing party simply because they believe in equality and do not consider that they have a right to be richer than the rest of the population: the rationality of this choice is that by voting for the left they feel better and therefore achieve some personal gain. But if one is to take into account all these forms of rational behaviour, then any motivation may indeed be rational. Clearly, it is not possible as yet to consider all motivations; and it is probably right in practice to concentrate on some of the more obvious rational standpoints. But it seems also possible to broaden and take into account habits of various kinds, which do in fact exert a considerable influence in various political processes, specifically in voting: many vote for a party because they have voted for it in the past and associate this party with such general aims as, for instance, the interests of the working class and the common people, even though it might be shown that such a party did not, as a matter of fact, help the common people in a number of cases.

In fact the basis of rational-choice models has already been broadened to contain a variety of habits and practices which may be technically irrational but are in fact quite common. But it is difficult to see how these models could be extended to cover the third and most serious problem which political scientists have to face, namely, the very constraints under which society operates. It is possible to suggest that habits are somehow rational, but what about potential 'drives' and 'urges' which emerge either slowly or violently and might change the motivations of actors? What if some political actors become convinced that they cannot achieve their goals (which they believe to be good, *ex hypothesi*) and, instead of being 'rational' and being prepared to consider them as dreams, what if they try to break the constraints under which the system operates? A model might be able to examine the strength of a number of tensions within society and warn about the dangers of break-up, but the conditions of political life become so different after the danger point that rational-choice models, or even 'post rational-choice' models appear virtually functionless. Yet – and this is the crux of the matter – a large part of political activity consists in just such dreaming about a new reality (as we saw in the preceding chapter); its importance cannot be denied, however unlikely the dreams are to be implemented.

We are here once more confronted with the problems of structures and of their role in the analysis of political life. Even models that go beyond rational choice can only take the existence of structures into account – they cannot go beyond them. When we consider the effect of collective action, in contrast with two-person or small-group bargaining, we are simply taking more closely into consideration the effect which structures, and in particular procedures, may have on the solution of particular problems: this is therefore a more realistic presentation. Similarly, when we consider habits, we are in effect considering the role of structures, because institutional and procedural pressures produce habits: for example, people have the habit of voting for a political party; they are linked to the party through years of association; they would not 'dream' of voting for another existing party, let alone of voting for an altogether new party. This is to say that such 'post rational-choice' analyses can take into account the structures, but they cannot explain either why the structures exist, or the strength which these structures have. Sometimes they can help to determine which institution is most likely to achieve the desired result; since the models are operating on the basis of existing structures, they cannot, by definition, determine the solidity of those structures.

Thus behavioural theory does remain partial: it tends to explain how the system works, rather than the existence of the system itself; it has to be complemented by some form of investigation into structures. It is important, however, both in the results it has already achieved and in the direction which it has given to studies of politics, even if many still do not accept that models of political analysis have to become more formal and the approach to the study of behaviour more systematic. But behavioural theory is perhaps even more important because it gradually brings political scientists and the public closer together: perhaps many politicians still consider their 'intuition' to be more valuable than a complex analysis of sequences of decisions; but decisions have become so complex and their consequences so difficult to discover merely through 'intuition' that politicians, in many countries, and in the United States in particular, have come to recognize that a systematic examination of 'policy flows' is a necessity.

Thus the real debate relates not so much to the question of 'formalization', but to the approach this formalization should adopt: it centres on the question of the basic 'hypotheses', rational or not, which are introduced in the models of political behaviour. One should not be too prone to dismiss a 'rational-choice' approach: alternative models are not easily discovered, although it might seem simple to present 'general critiques' of society. As modern political analysis is engaged both in the development of rational-choice models and in a constant re-appraisal of these models, the future of behavioural theory seems promising; and political life – not merely political science – should benefit from this promise.

CHAPTER 7

Structural theory

In Chapter 3, we began noting the reasons why norms, structures and behaviour formed the three aspects of the inquiry in which political scientists were involved. Our examination of behavioural analysis, in the previous chapter, confirmed the existence of these three aspects. The study of structures – institutions, procedures, customs, existing arrangements of all kinds, however ill-applied – is one of the most important parts of the work of political scientists. Yet structural theory has perhaps an even lower status than behavioural theory. Political science has thus its highly paradoxical aspects: normative analysis cannot lead to effective prescription – to actual change – without a theory of behaviour; this theory of behaviour implies a theory of the structures within which the behaviour takes place. Political scientists seem to realize instinctively the existence of this paradox as they become involved in structural analyses; yet few are ready to deem as theory most of what is studied in the field of structures.

This state of affairs stems from a combination of two reasons. First, structural theory suffered from being too closely linked to legal theory. Studies of institutions grew first in the eighteenth and nineteenth centuries as a by-product of the study of constitutions: many institutions – legislatures, for instance – were created by constitutions; new relationships were created between these, and already existing institutions, such as executives and courts.[1] These developments were among the most

[1] This was what many of the great classics had been involved in for many generations previously, but more direct examples were Locke and Montesquieu, both of whom devised blueprints from which many features of the presidential and parliamentary systems were taken.

important in the rise of the liberal State, which owes its basic
framework, not merely to normative theory, but to the institutional theories that were 'invented' in order to implement principles. But constitutional theory did not cover or pay attention
to other political groupings, such as parties, or to groups which
have a political role, such as a variety of associations – the
bureaucracy, the military, the churches. Moreover, constitutional theory was somewhat unprepared to deal with countries
which did not have a liberal system of government: as long as it
was assumed – as it was during much of the nineteenth century –
that liberal institutions would spread gradually and evenly, the
problem was small, but when traditional States of an autocratic
nature either perpetuated themselves or turned into autocracies
of a new type, the problem became more serious. Disaffection
with constitutional theory grew from the increasing realization
of an apparently unbridgeable gap between law and reality. We
saw in Chapter 3 the reasons why the gap is not as unbridgeable
as some may believe and why political scientists have to take
into account both legal structures and their implementation.
The analysis of structures has tended to be a partial theory
comprising legal analyses and the 'hard aspects of the reality'
which seemed intractable to any theory. The influence of the
historical school has been strongly felt: the examination of the
many cases in which historical events seemed to undermine the
constitutional models led to the conclusion that the study of
institutions could be only piecemeal, not systematic, empirical
or theoretical, and almost entirely inductive rather than deductive.

   Another root of the problem lies in the very efforts that were
made to re-introduce systematic analyses by by-passing institutions altogether: structural theory seemed overtaken and about
to be replaced by a more continuous or general analysis of political life. The search for a deductive theory and for means of
studying continuous forms of change distracted attention from
structures and in particular from structures of individual countries. The understanding of the operation of forces, such as
power, bargaining and communication seemed ultimately to
help to identify the 'real' variables designed in turn to explain
the concrete structures. Viewed from this angle, structural analysis appeared less important, indeed derivative: only to be

undertaken at a second stage. Meanwhile, studies of institutions seemed to involve more anecdotes than fundamental research. In the same way as economic theory can by-pass the study of structures, at least to a large extent, political analysis could seemingly ultimately by-pass institutions and be based on the systematic study of the political relationships between individuals or groups.

This effort is unlikely ever to be successful, as we saw in the previous chapter. But, meanwhile, not enough emphasis has been placed by political scientists on the study of institutions and procedures as the necessary 'macro' element which links the various aspects of political life, connects the present with the past and constitutes the framework within which 'micro' behaviour takes place. Too much emphasis has been placed on legal and historical considerations. A number of political scientists did analyse structural problems beyond the confines of constitutional theory and were concerned to incorporate 'reality' in their analyses. But perhaps because of the prevalence of behavioural analyses and of the behavioural endeavour, this structural theory has too often seemed related exclusively to a particular school of thought, namely 'structural-functionalism', which is only *one* model of analysis and gives only one view of the political system; indeed it is more a model of the political system than a theory.

We are not concerned here with the discussion of only one of the theories. We are not even primarily involved in describing the various theories (or models) of political scientists in relation to structures, any more than we were in relation to norms and behaviour: we are concerned with exploring the processes of mind which lead political scientists to analyse certain phenomena in a certain way. We need to discuss all approaches equally, whether it is systematic or historical, whether it aim or not at reducing institutions to behavioural variables, or whether it is based or not on particular functions of structures in the political system. Although we refer here to *structural theory*, we do not refer to any one particular theory of structures, but are concerned with the object of the study and the way in which it is in fact considered by political thinkers.

As in the previous two chapters, we shall begin by examining the preliminary process by which students of politics approach

the question of structures. We need not restate the reasons which
emerged in the course of the previous chapter and which make
the study of structures a necessity; but we should also remember
the prescriptive reasons which lead necessarily to the study of
institutions: if principles are to be applied, the possible ways of
implementing them must be considered. We shall start from this
point and see what difficulties arise, in particular when such
views come to be confronted with piecemeal descriptions of
individual institutions on grounds of 'realism'. We shall then
examine the process of analysis: classification is difficult, and
'continuous' studies are often precluded, because cases are too
few. This is why *comparisons* have come to be an end in themselves
– and comparative methods or theories are sometimes viewed as
co-extensive with theories of structures. We shall then consider
some of the end-products and and see how the study of structures contributes to our understanding of politics alongside
normative and behavioural theories.

I.   *The starting point of structural analysis*
   A. *Legal, historical and sociological approaches to the analysis of
structures.* As soon as someone wishes to achieve a better organization of society, he proposes that a law, regulation or order be
altered. And, if he does not feel contented with the basic
arrangements of the country in which he lives, he proposes
changes in the constitution. Students of politics are also concerned, almost automatically, with changes in laws and constitutions, because they, too, believe naturally that one way (perhaps the quickest way) of providing a solution to difficulties is by
amendment of the legal arrangements which are in force.
Structural theory is therefore naturally and very closely associated to legal developments: laws, in the broadest sense, including constitutions and the most detailed regulations, are the
mechanism by which reforms can be achieved (or the *status quo*
maintained).

   This link between politics and law may or may not be satisfying to everyone; many may feel that laws are cumbersome
arrangements; they might prefer other mechanisms. But the
link does exist. Yet institutions and procedures do not only stem
from legal documents: they are also the product of 'tradition';
they are embedded in the history of the nation. Everyone senses

intuitively that there are institutions which fit 'well' with the general customs of the nation, while other institutions, perhaps imported from outside, are 'superimposed'.

History and tradition are therefore another starting point of structural theory; but they give also a different character to structures. Legal analysis suggests a clear-cut definition of institutions and procedures; tradition, on the contrary, suggests greater vagueness. Changes in laws helps to date the moment when institutions are altered; tradition leads to smooth and imperceptible modifications. While laws lead to a possible universal application of a principle, tradition stresses the unique characteristics of the context in which institutions are born and develop.

But law and history are not the only origins of structural theory in politics. When we consider institutions that are the product of tradition, we soon notice that there are many similarities between the traditions of various nations. And we also notice that a number of institutions develop and have many characteristics in common. It is true that political parties in a particular country owe much to tradition and need to be studied historically: but it is also true that these parties have many common features, not only between themselves, but with political parties in other countries. For instance, they organize the population towards elections; they select leaders; they propose programmes. And political parties seem to owe their strength to social forces which play a large part in the community or in the nation: everywhere in Western Europe, for instance, working class movements have led to the development of socialist parties; in many countries, religious groups, and Catholic groups in particular, have been at the origin of political parties.

Nor is this all: even the institutions which are created by laws and constitutions seem to evolve as a result of various social forces. The constitution may state what Parliament will do: the practice may (and probably will) turn out to be very different. Although the legal origin of these institutions is important – and although those who are concerned with structural analysis have to look carefully at their legal powers – they have also to be concerned with the study of the developments which have taken place since the institution was created. To take an example: everywhere in Western Europe, the role of the executive has

increased and the legislature tends to adopt the proposals made
by the government. The study of constitutions would not
explain this phenomenon; nor can a purely historical approach
truly account for this characteristic which is common to all
modern industrial countries. We have to turn to an examination
of the types of social forces that exist nowadays in industrial
countries. This is why a sociological approach is as necessary to
the study of structures as a legal and an historical approach. A
comprehensive analysis of structures thus entails a combination
of legal, historical and sociological analysis.

B. *Detailed and global approaches to the study of structures. The notion
of political system.* Of the three starting points of structural analysis, history is the one which stresses especially the need to look
at structures, not in isolation, but in the context of all the structures of the country. But it would be wrong to suppose that
lawyers or sociologists are concerned only with individual
structures. Strictly, the determination of the powers of a legislature, for instance, entails relating legislatures to other bodies,
such as the executive, or the judiciary. Powers are by definition
relative; they specify that a particular institution will be concerned with some matters – which means that another will not,
or that two will share these powers. Consequently, if it is felt that
an institution needs to be improved, and if it is suggested that
this be done by a change in the law, it is necessary to look at the
overall implications of the change for all the other (or at least
many other) institutions in the country. This is indeed why the
classical theorists who were particularly concerned with
changes in political institutions, such as Locke or Montesquieu,
looked for and genuinely invented theories of the relationship
between powers of government, such as the theory of the 'separation of powers' (which assigns specific functions to the legislature, the executive and the judiciary and thereby organizes a
particular relationship between these bodies). And the same
could be said of sociologists who have been concerned with, for
instance, the relative role of political parties and other groups,
or the relative role of parties and the bureaucracy. Whether they
approach the study of institutions and procedures from an
historical, a legal, or a sociological angle, structural theorists
have been concerned with inter-relationships: they have been
concerned with the determination of the balance between

various parts of a *political system*.

Yet this interest in the whole system conflicts with many of the aims of political thinkers and strains the capabilities of their tools. While historically minded political scientists may stress the need for a contextual approach, this approach is so general that it soon seems to lead to unrealistic standpoints. And while legalists and sociologists may in theory believe in the inter-relationships between all parts of the system, the mind boggles at the difficulties which such a premise creates for the analysis. It may, of course, be argued that the problem of isolating an element from the whole must arise in other disciplines; but either this isolation can be done by way of contrived experiments, as in the natural sciences, or there are definite means of establishing relationships, as in economics, where money (normally) pro-vides a useful medium. In a political system, it seems more difficult to concentrate on one element (whether it be an insti-tution or a procedure) and test it by varying the conditions in the environment.

Thus, not only is the starting point of the inquiry diffuse; the problems which are posed seem to lead to almost insoluble difficulties. We began discussing normative theory in Chapter 5 by noting that there was seemingly no way of deducing all the principles from a common source: the principles, or problems, are 'facts' in the landscape; interconnections have to be tried out, often with limited success. The problem is at least as serious – and somewhat similar – for the student of structures: he has to proceed while having regard to structures of a varied character, which are inter-related in various ways and which often bear a misleading similarity. So it is not surprising that a comprehen-sive structural theory should have been slow to develop; nor that it should be divided into so many schools of thought. 'Institu-tional' theory in the legalistic sense has markedly advanced, but it remains too closely associated to the analysis of purely legal arrangements. Historians have paid attention to the background in which institutions have grown, but have often exaggerated the importance of different cultural contexts. Sociologically inclined political thinkers have leapt towards grand theory often at the expense of empirical content and concrete explanation. The healthy development of structural theory implies the combination of various approaches; the common concern of those who think politically seems indeed to lead new research in such a direction, as can increasingly be seen by the unco-ordinated but lively development of comparative work which has been the main means of analysis in the field of structures.

II. *The process of development of structural theory: the role of comparative analyses*

Not always consciously perhaps, political scientists concerned with the analysis of structures quickly become aware of the complex character of the problems that they tackle. This is why, out of the gamut of methodologies that we described in Chapter 4, they have searched for some method of coping with structures by steering a middle course between the various extremes. As there are various types of structures which can seemingly be distinguished and related (parties and legislatures, for example) classification seems the obvious first step; as there are idiosyncratic characteristics of each individual structure, they have tried to tackle problems by describing cases. This has enabled them to look at the same type of structure, not only over space, but over time as well. From this (instinctive) recognition of movements over time stemmed also the effort to tackle problems of development and decay of the various structures. Perhaps the combination of these elements, with differing emphasis from individual observers, does not deserve to be labelled a 'method'. Partly because it has usefully grappled with the problems, and partly because it is so widespread among students of structures, it has acquired in effect the status of a method: to a very large extent, structural analysis has become shaped and moulded by a complex, flexible, but also recognizable battery of tools: this is what is understood as the comparative method in the study of structures.

A. *The analysis of structures and its basic 'comparative' component.* If structures are 'things', and 'things' of different sizes and kinds, how can they be analysed, dissected and understood? If they were unique, they should be studied separately, and the best type of method would be a description of each case. But structures are not truly unique. First, their uniqueness is different from the uniqueness of events, such as the French Revolution or the Second World War: they continue over time; over a period, they both remain the same and change. If anything, they are more like unique men than unique events; but, unlike great men, they are related to other similar structures either existing concurrently or at different periods. Similarities exist because of imitation of other political systems, and also because of a certain common development which can be discerned in the way men deal with some problems, so we find that parliamentary or presidential systems of government in many countries were imported, and we also find disparate countries producing analogous structures such as executives, courts and procedures. Because of these two characteristics of structures, there is an inbuilt tendency for students of structures to go beyond cases and move towards comparisons.

This tendency is natural; it corresponds to the peculiar character of the objects which are being studied. Yet it is far from being always consciously practised in the study of all institutions and procedures, because of the pull exercised by the need for facts and the desire to describe situations as concretely as possible. Many studies of structures are, indeed, ostensibly – even perhaps aggressively – studies of cases. A large number of works aim at describing one, and only one structure; they represent perhaps the majority of all studies of structures: they might concentrate on the American Senate, the Socialist Party of Germany, the French bureaucracy or the British Cabinet, and many cases are even devoted to the examination of structures which are much less renowned and would seem to be only of interest to narrow specialists.

Much of this effort may seem at first sight to contradict the requirements of comparative work. The reason for it lies with the limitations of data collection. The structures of organizations are sometimes concealed – for example, with many 'elevated' decision bodies, such as cabinets.[2] They often are little known, as are most structures of new countries. Yet the comparative study depends on the ability to assess carefully the differences in organization between various bodies, the types of programmes presented by parties, the forms of decision-making adopted by executives.

[2] See in particular R. H. S. Crossman's Introduction to a new edition of Bagehot's classic, *The English Constitution* (Fontana Library edition, London, 1963), pp. 1-57.

Comparisons may thus often not be the direct object of study; but the existence of structures simply makes it impossible to abandon for long the comparative aspect. A study of the British Cabinet implies some generalizations about executives, whether explicit or not.

Not surprisingly, the comparative approach has become almost second nature to those who study structures. Part of their training is geared to alerting those concerned with institutions and procedures to similarities and differences. Originally, legal analyses led to the development of many categories – separation of powers, parliamentary systems, representative government, for instance. This became later enlarged in order to include other institutions which had not been created through laws and constitutions; such as one- or two-party systems. This led to comparisons between complex situations. The comparative method is of course not limited to political science and to studies of structures, but nowhere perhaps is it as crucial to the analysis itself.

Naturally enough, since comparisons are always implicit, they are often made explicit. Sometimes they are merely used as illustrations, sometimes they are given a central role. Comparative government and comparative politics naturally became important sub-fields taught in universities, though it is often not recognized that it is the study of structures, and not comparison per se, which is the real field of study. One starts, perhaps, with a simple description of a structure; in the course of the examination, however, one may realize that the same structure has a comparable role in another country. From a consideration, say, of the British Labour Party, one is led to look at socialist parties in other European countries, and to consider all, or at least many socialist parties. As one generalizes, one must note the differences: there are small and large parties, parties with different ideologies, parties with different organizations; some operate in a pluralistic context, while others exist in single-party systems. One is gradually embarking on a structural theory of parties, as one would also be if one were studying any other structure.

But the comparative method remains flexible: it allows those who wish to generalize to remain close to the facts and thus to steer a middle course between the approaches. The level of comparison is partly dictated by the nature of the problem, the knowledge which has been acquired, and the requirements of greater intellectual unity. Thus the comparative method makes for compromises which may seem inelegant, but are a practical way of dealing with the variables. If one cannot compare all parties, one can reduce the scope to, say, Western democracies. If differences between legislatures or courts across the world are too large as a result of different ideologies or different social structures, one can concentrate on more limited comparisons.

B. *The search for a yardstick and the problem of functional equivalence.* Yet the comparative method solves only one aspect of the problem. How can it help us when we try to assess inter-relationships? It needs to be refined if more than one structure is under the microscope. Indeed, even in studies of one structure, we find ourselves quickly involved in problems of relations. Suppose that we are interested in political parties: their number, organization and programmes vary markedly, and in some countries, they do not even exist at all. How is our comparison to proceed? It would be tedious, and not very productive, simply to describe successively all the parties that exist in the world. The inquiry may need such a dictionary as an intermediate phase; but it cannot be its end-product. We must put some order in the analysis if we are to satisfy ourselves that we can understand the economy of the arrangements and if we are to be able to draw some lessons. But how will it be possible to discover some order? We have to find a universal yardstick, against which to measure political parties – though it is not so much a question of strict measurement as of categorization.

For a very long time, the question was avoided because the legal yardstick drawn from the classical theorists and from the economy of constitutions seemed to be self-evident. If the whole universe under observation has the same goals, there is little incentive to discover what these goals are. Eighteenth- and nineteenth-century theorists did invent a number of constitutional systems, such as the parliamentary and presidential systems, as well as 'variations' of these systems; but these systems all had the same goals, namely the achievement of the liberalization of the State. It is true that many countries did not have liberal constitutions; but, at least up to the end of the nineteenth century, it was assumed that these countries would eventually

become liberal. It seemed therefore idle to consider the organization of regimes which were regarded as being on the verge of
disappearing. To take a precise example: the liberal system of
government appeared to entail the creation of a legislature or
parliament; why should one consider the relationships between
institutions in countries which did not have parliaments if one
felt that all countries would eventually have a parliament? Thus
legal categories seemed for a very long time a sufficient yardstick
for comparisons.

When it became clear, on the contrary, that the goal of a
liberal State was being increasingly challenged by new regimes,
particularly communist regimes, which did not intend to organize the powers of the various organs of the state according to the
canons of classical institutional theorists, the problem of a common yardstick became a practical necessity. Later, it appeared
that the institutions of the liberal State were changing under the
influence of social forces which had not been taken into consideration when the liberal constitutional model was invented –
for instance as a result of the emergence of parties and of many
new pressure groups. It had simply become impossible to avoid
a very long detour into the discovery of the role played by institutions in the general political system.

Let us take again the example of political parties. Let us pre-
sume that we do not at first wish to be involved in a global
discussion of the relationship between parties and the rest of the
structures of government, for instance, because such a study
would be too complex and would probably not lead us quickly
to a 'practical' study of our main object of analysis, the political
parties. We could, admittedly, draw a list of the characteristics
of political parties; we could say that we will compare parties
according to their size, to their number, to their type of leadership, to their programme or ideology. But we would soon have to
recognize that we could not avoid going beyond parties. How
could we begin to decide which of the elements in this list is the
'most important' unless we had some idea of the role of parties in
the political system as a whole? Moreover, when looking at the
world as a whole, we would have to note that some countries
have parties while others do not; that some have had parties in
the past and no longer have any, or *vice versa*. How are we to
handle such cases? Are we to say that we will simply consider the

countries which have parties now, and leave all other countries aside? But we would at least have to look at the reasons for the emergence of parties in some countries: and this would in-exorably lead us to the question of the broader context of the political system.

So we do have to look at the political system as a whole in order to find a yardstick by which to categorize the various structures. What can this yardstick be? Our reflections on the nature of the problem with which we are faced suggest at least one avenue that we could explore: we have, in the course of the last few pages, referred to the *role* that an institution, such as the political party, might have in the political system as a whole. It is as if the political system was composed of a number of ele-ments, each of which has some part to play. Various analogies spring naturally to mind: these are drawn for instance from the language of engineering – or, to be more modern, from the lan-guage of computing. We can imagine that the political system is a large machine designed to turn into policies (laws, regulations, but also governmental actions in general) the various pressures which come from special groups or from political parties. We can refer to 'inputs' (the proposals of the groups and parties) and to 'outputs' (the decisions which are adopted by the government).[3] But this is of course only an analogy; the danger is that, if the reality of political life is only similar to the activity of a computer, we might get carried away with our analogies. Not surprisingly, indeed, major controversies have arisen: some suggested comparisons based on the functions that structures fulfil in the overall network. They have been criticized on the grounds that the anthropomorphic language is not suitable, that a word such as function is too closely associated with what humans achieve. Yet the idea has value: it facilitates the exam-ination of possible equivalents to structures (for example, if there are no political parties, one would look for other groups performing a similar function) and also the comparison be-tween structures.[4]

[3] The description of the political system in terms of 'inputs' and 'outputs' was due in particular to D. Easton who came to be one of the major proponents of the 'systems approach'; see *A Systems Analysis of Political Life* (Wiley, New York, 1965).

[4] This effort was attempted in particular by G. A. Almond. See G. A. Almond

This approach is fraught with difficulties; it is better as a general idea than as a concrete tool. The difficulties lie in the precise evaluation of the exact roles or functions of particular structures: the words used and methods of measurement are vague. A yardstick is also needed to compare the effectiveness of the various structures; but what comes to be done is that an attempt is made to provide explanations as well as comparisons. Parties are not simply described as structures helping to aggregate the views of the people into common programmes; they are also described as means by which the system is sustained or supported. They may well do this as well, but this is no longer a function in the detailed sense, which can be contrasted with another function fulfilled by the same structure or another structure; it is an explanation of how the political system, first, *may* operate and second, remains stable, as if a hidden hand helped to keep together the various pieces of an intricate machine. At the moment there is no way of distinguishing operations which take place in a nation and the more comprehensive functions which contribute to the maintenance of the system.

III.   *The end-products of structural theory*
Some of these end-products are concerned with whole political systems since the structural-functional approach has been preoccupied with finding a yardstick by which to measure and give explanations for given configurations in given polities. But much structural analysis also takes place on the plane of 'middle-range' analysis, which some indeed consider to be the only plane where real progress is achieved – at least at the present level of development of structural theory.

A. *Middle-range analyses.* Middle-range analysis characterizes studies which go beyond a specific case, but remain concerned with a particular structure, the direct relationship between structures, or the relationship between structures in a given

and J. S. Coleman, *The politics of the developing areas,* and G. A. Almond and G. B. Powell, *Comparative Politics.* But the problem of operationalization of functions was not solved and criticisms were made about the ideological content of what was in the first instance a methodological approach. See below, Section 3 of this chapter. See also J. Blondel, *Introduction to Comparative Government* (Weidenfeld and Nicolson, London, 1969), Chapters 2 and 3, pp. 15-42.

context (perhaps with a certain type of political system). Of course, many case-studies, even many historical studies, come close to middle-range analyses. If the British Cabinet is studied since the early nineteenth century, the work may be historical; but it is also a middle-range analysis, as it identifies some of the variables which account, for instance, for the development of the power of the prime minister and thus help to distinguish between the role of personalities and the role of structures.

Much political analysis in the 'great classics' is normative; but we also saw that much is descriptive: much is in fact middle-range structural analysis. Constitutional and legal analyses, as well as broader structural analyses, from Aristotle to Bagehot, through Machiavelli, Hobbes, Locke, Montesquieu, Rousseau, Burke, the Federalists, Tocqueville and Mill, have been concerned with the establishment of political laws. It was Montesquieu who claimed that he was looking for the 'laws' or 'invariant' relationships in matters of social behaviour.[5] The idea of discovering social laws related to structures has been criticized (among others, by some political scientists) as being an impossible task, one that directly results from the influence of modern science on the social sciences. This is quite mistaken: Aristotle related institutions to types of government; Machiavelli unfolded the conditions under which certain types of rule could become effective; Montesquieu discussed, after Locke, the institutions which were to serve as a base for modern 'liberal' government; Rousseau proposed various institutions to promote democracy. These thinkers were often more concerned with structures than they were with behaviour. Machiavelli, Hobbes and Mill were those who were most concerned with behaviour itself; but much of their analysis is at the intermediate level between the global analysis of the political system and daily behaviour; they were perhaps the main protagonists of what has become modern middle-range structural theory.

In recent decades, many aspects of the political system have been examined at this middle-range level. One area which came to be particularly important before World War II was that of the relationship between electoral systems and party systems, because it seemed plausible to argue that proportional representation had the effect of creating large numbers of small

[5] See Chapter 3, p. 34.

parties and thus, indirectly, of making governments less stable in parliamentary systems. After many political scientists considered the problem in its various aspects, it became clearer that the relationships between electoral systems and party systems was not as close as was once envisaged. But there is some relationship: two-party systems do tend to be associated with 'majority' systems on the British model, though other factors also contribute to the number and relative size of parties.

But the study of the links between elections and parties is only one part, and indeed a very small part, of the work which is concerned with the elaboration of middle-range theory. One field which has attracted much attention is that of authoritarian rule, and in particular of military rule. We now know the conditions under which a military regime is likely to be established, as well as the likelihood of such a regime maintaining itself. The relationship between executive and legislature is also better known: it is becoming clear that the powers of the cabinet, in a parliamentary system, lead directly to the decrease in the independence of the legislature. Presidential systems are more likely to preserve the strength of the legislature (a good example is the United States), but the strength and personal authority of the president may also often be such that the result can be a somewhat chaotic government and that there is a danger of collapse of the regime – a point which brings us nearer to global analyses. In a different field, the control of technicians by the political class has been observed to lead to a reduction in the dynamism of the bureaucracy and so one can only optimize between control and dynamism, not maximize both aspects in any polity.[6]

These examples demonstrate that generalizations are not only possible but that they are gradually made more precise as new cases give a better and more comprehensive picture of the panorama of structures in political systems. But conclusions are

[6] The controversy about the relationship between electoral systems and party systems has been very extensive and lasted over a generation, as it has been asserted that proportional representation led to many parties, many parties to governmental instability and governmental instability to regime collapse (i.e. Weimar). This theory was propounded by F. Hermens, *Democracy or Anarchy* (U. of Notre Dame Press, South Bend, Indiana, 1940). It was developed at length by M. Duverger in *Political Parties* (Methuen, London, 1955). For the most recent and most sophisticated treatment of the subject see D. Rae, *The political consequences of electoral laws* (Yale U.P., New Haven, 1967). On the

often hampered by limited data; and the data collected are often presented in ways which make comparisons difficult and give rise to criticisms from those more inclined to favour detailed analyses of concrete situations. The military, the bureaucracy and perhaps parties (and electoral systems) are the types of structures which have been most amenable to middle-range analysis: partly because these structures are the most universal and the most homogeneous and partly because data have been easier to obtain and thus more naturally attracted the attention of observers. Governmental structures, legislatures, courts and even many groups have remained under-studied, at least at middle-range level, most of the examination remaining particular and being only middle-range in its historical bent. Perhaps the development of middle-range theory needs to be more spectacular to attract attention and to incite more scholars to devote their activities to this intermediate level: until then, findings will remain limited and the data base insufficient.

B. *The study of political systems.* As long as middle-range theory remains somewhat inconclusive, much of the resources of political thinking are likely to be devoted to the study of whole political systems: not only is the study of whole political systems important in itself, but also many scholars are not content to remain at a level which does not provide a global understanding of society. It may appear 'scientifically' unreasonable to study the whole while the detailed parts are insufficiently known, but there is pressure towards broader studies within political science itself from normative theorists, who suggest and develop remedies, and from politicians and the public, who want explanations and look for remedies.

The dividing line between middle-range and grander theory is also difficult to draw, for instance in a case where the breakdown of structures suggests the existence of basic oppositions in society. Structural theory has been concerned to delineate the basic relationships between a variety of structures which

extent to which the military is constrained by events, and in particular by the need to 'civilianize' itself, see S. E. Finer, *The Man on Horseback* (Pall Mall, London, 1962), *passim,* and in particular pp. 14-22 and 240-43. On the role of technicians and their problems, see J. Blondel, *op. cit.,* pp. 391-412. These are only given as examples of some of the types of generalizations which have consciously been made in this field.

contribute to form what might be termed – perhaps with some exaggeration – a 'harmonious' political system. The harmony, in this sense, is internal and does not necessarily correspond to the desires and urges of either political thinkers or much of the public. If the political system is conceived of as a computer, which processes demands and turns them into laws or other end-products, one can see how structures may serve different functions depending on the particular system. In one situation parties may act as pressure groups by processing popular demands; elsewhere they may act as legislatures by studying and vetting laws; yet elsewhere they may even – as in some single-party States – act to control and educate the public, as the military or the police. So, as the analysis proceeds, a variety of 'functional equivalents' are found and analysed, enlarging the range of the possible alternatives (though these alternatives will neither be infinite nor completely random).[7]

Once prescriptive principles and goals have been formulated to the satisfaction of political thinkers and the general public then the conditions under which these goals may be implemented have still to be studied. This raises at one level questions of stability and maintenance of structures – or of the structural arrangements – which exist in a given polity at a given point in time; it leads at another to discussing the conditions under which different arrangements would both provide 'better' results and would survive without causing problems for the political system. Let us assume that both middle-range theory and a combination of middle-range analyses have made it possible to suggest what types of arrangements would ideally implement the given prescriptive aims: the study of political systems thus leads to an examination of conditions under which structures relate to populations by being 'acceptable', 'tolerated' or 'rejected'.

The question of the conditions promoting the stability of political systems has long exercised students of politics. The notion of 'legitimacy' has thus been used; first it was confined to the right which kings and other monarchs might have to be lawful leaders and to their chances of being 'tolerated'; gradually the concept was extended to cover all political systems

[7] See D. Easton, *op. cit.*, and G. A. Almond, and G. B. Powell, *op. cit.*

which seemed to require, in order to be maintained, some form of at least passive support from the whole or a large section of the population. As the legitimacy of kings depended in part on their family claims and partly on their ability to meet the demands of the polity (in particular not to disturb well-established habits and privileges), the legitimacy of political systems came to be seen as dependent on time and on their adaptability in response to demands. On the one hand, structures which exist tend to be recognized, at least passively; habits are formed around them. The behaviour which we analysed in the previous chapter thus depends on structures and procedures; similarly, the fact that citizens wish to see general social conditions remain predictable and orderly enhances the 'legitimacy' of many institutions and political systems.[8]

But there are cases when this basic legitimacy can be markedly reduced. Perhaps the effectiveness of the structures diminishes: either because institutions may not be harmoniously related; or because new demands may render inadequate some of the structures as when there is an increased demand for economic development or social equality. Political scientists have been concerned with an examination of the conditions which produce such high tension that the political system is no longer viable. The development of new forms of 'populist' political systems in much of the Third World, based on one-party systems or on the military, is evidence of the apparent inadequacy of many traditional monarchical or oligarchical systems to cope with the new demands of modern society. Evidence also shows that liberal democracies tend, on the whole, to be more stable in those parts of the world where socio-economic development is higher. The analysis of the conditions for the maintenance of political systems is thus an important part of structural theory.

Less developed is the second side of the analysis – that of the conditions under which a system *can acquire* enough legitimacy to achieve its results while maintaining itself. If a system is new, it is likely to undergo strains, since the configuration of structures has to become accepted, and new habits have to be

[8] The analysis of the 'conditions' of democracy and in particular of stable democracy has given rise to many studies. See in particular S. E. Lipset, *op. cit.*, Chapters 2 and 3, for one of the earliest systematic presentations of the problem and of the evidence.

formed; older habits will not disappear overnight and they will therefore naturally increase tension in the political system. This is why it appears necessary both to use coercion and to attempt to 'educate' the mass of the citizens. Gradually, models that define the conditions under which political systems can undergo change are being made more precise: there appears to be a limit to the amount of coercion which systems can sustain; thus there is a limit to the extent of change which can in fact be enforced. However unacceptable the previous system and even if, as was the case in the French and Russian Revolutions, much of the population appears actively or at least passively to support the new system, change cannot be introduced without imposing new structures, thus creating difficulties for the political system.[9]

With 'legitimacy', 'coercion' or 'imposition', we encounter concepts which like those discussed in normative and behavioural theory, are potentially continuous, rather than dichotomous, and yet difficult to measure because of the characteristics of the political material to which they are applied. Indeed, to quite a remarkable extent, it is possible to use in connection with these concepts elements of analysis which come, by way of economics, from physics or mathematics. It is not impossible to compare legitimacy to a form of capital, which, once accumulated, allows a political leader or, in an abstract sense, a political system to make expenditures in the form of applying pressure to people and extracting obedience. Systems which are new and which, as a result, have scarcely been able to accumulate a 'capital' of legitimacy from the population are more vunerable to the tensions which daily disagreements are bound to create: they may 'borrow', for instance, some element of strength from popular leaders:[10] or they

[9] The literature on 'political development' is large and it consists both of detailed and middle-range studies and of general works. Among the latter, see D. E. Apter, *The politics of modernization* (University of Chicago Press, 1965), in which the conditions of imposition are analysed.

[10] The role of personalities was mentioned at first by Max Weber who suggested that 'charismatic' rule was important alongside traditional and bureaucratic rule. The role of personalities has been studied very widely, often on the basis of case-studies, but sometimes more generally. See on this subject D. E. Apter, *op. cit.,* pp. 359 and ff.

may manipulate the 'credit system' by introducing compulsion, but at the expense (as through inflation) of their future maintenance.

For the moment it is still unrealistic to expect the development of a general theory which would turn these analogies into a precise set of laws. But the analyses at least indicate broad characteristics under which whole political systems do in fact emerge, grow and die. They confirm the ambiguous character with which political thinking is 'condemned' to approach the study of political reality. This ambiguity lies not only in the mind of the political thinker, but in the very material with which he is concerned. When considering normative theory, we saw that descriptive analyses were both a necessity and also a constraint on the development of many utopias. When analysing whole political systems, we find again the connections between norms and structures. We do not know precisely how long it will take for a new law to transform old habits into a new mould: but we know that it will take time, that the more removed that law is from existing habits the more difficult it will be for the law to be obeyed; compulsion or disobedience will therefore be inevitable with a new legal rule which tries to change markedly the codes of behaviour. What applies for a law will apply even more for a whole set of rules, a whole normative framework being presented to a society. It is not surprising that 'revolutionary' change should be rarer than is sometimes stated, hoped for, or feared: the Chinese cultural revolution was a typical attempt to impose a whole set of structures, which proved to be very 'expensive' in political (and indeed financial and human) terms; for this reason such cultural revolutions have seldom happened and will always be rare in the history of mankind.

Structural theory is inchoate: some may say that it has been so for such a long time that it is unlikely to improve dramatically in the course of the next few years, or even decades. At the middle-range, not enough efforts have perhaps been made to collect data of a truly precise character. At the 'grander' level, the difficulties of 'operationalization' stem from the material itself: a pattern of structures cannot be easily summarized in a precise language, though, as with some aspects of behavioural theory, the development of a mathematics based on patterns, rather than numbers, might help in the future; a second stage might consist of charting the rate at which given changes in structural configurations (and by implication, in normative systems) become acceptable to a population.

Although structural theory is nowhere near this stage, it is contributing to an understanding of the conditions of change; it helps by specifying those changes which are likely to take place without endangering the system (if this is feared to be a danger) and those changes which are likely to require an alteration of the configuration of structures if they are to be implemented. The analysis also specifies that changes in structural configurations will require some 'energy' or 'compulsion', and might indeed in the process involve the breakdown of the system. We began considering theory at the level of norms, and saw that structures were the only means by which new norms could be introduced (or older norms maintained); on the other hand, structures are also maintained by norms, because the decay of systems is related, as we saw, to the presence of new demands which the older structures are unable to accommodate. But structures also have a life of their own; they follow a cycle, mysterious in part, yet exerting much influence: by shaping the habits of citizens; by limiting the actions of political leaders who remain wary of tampering with them; by continuing to fascinate political scientists.

CHAPTER 8

Thinking politically

Our itinerary through the processes of thought of those who are concerned with the analyses of norms, of behaviour and of structures has revealed many of the differences that we were expecting; but it has also revealed the interconnections that we anticipated in Chapters 3 and 4, when we looked at the common concern and at the many common methods of approach – if not techniques – which characterize those who think politically. Too much emphasis has been placed on the divisions between the different schools of political thought, which merely leads to antagonism. Normative theorists are involved in much description of old and new structures, and in many hypotheses about the behaviour of individual actors. We saw that behavioural analyses have to remain at the micro level, because they cannot avoid the structures which form the framework of much of politics; and that structural analysis cannot account for behaviour at the micro-level. Some observers may be more concerned with the broad movements which affect societies and change the basic framework in which these operate; but the framework of broad structures, and even the detailed arrangements within these structures cannot and will not tell us how best to maximize our short-term goals. Most people have short-term goals that they cannot and will not abandon for the benefit of long-term ends. Those who think politically must, if they are to give serious attention to the whole of politics, be able to understand and account for both these short-term goals and the broader problems that structures can create.

Thinking politically is a broad and vast enterprise; so vast that no one political scientist can ever be expected to 'think politically' in the widest possible sense. He may have some idea of the overall landscape; he may recognize that there are, over there, some mountains, lakes and seas with which he should be more familiar. But if he is a climber, probably neither his training nor his inclination will be strong enough to impel him towards becoming a sailor. Yet it is a narrow political scientist who does not have any idea of the problems that confront the whole discipline, of the nature of the planes on which thinking has to take place.

Let us look therefore once more at what kind of man thinking politically does create and what kinds of conditions it imposes on the whole profession and on each of its members. Let us do so, not by looking at aspects, or approaches, as we had to do while introducing the subject, but by looking at what those who think politically are likely to be aware of. Our examination of the subject reveals five main points, which are mostly interrelated, but which need separate treatment because each of them gives to thinking politically a slightly different twist. They are 'modes of thinking', almost attitudes of mind; individually they are not peculiar to political thought, but the combination of them probably is.

I. *Accepting the diversity of political events with modesty*

First, thinking politically does require, and will always require, more modesty than other sciences. It may become a physicist to be arrogant about what he does: he can tell others how physical objects are related to each other. It may become an economist to show arrogantly the underlying mechanics of our monetary relations. It becomes historians, perhaps, to speak arrogantly about the misdeeds (and successes) of the dead. Those who think politically have to be more modest.

The reason is not that they are dealing with the activities of the powerful, who might prevent them from expressing their thoughts, but they have to practise a little modesty because those in power may simply be 'great people'. They have to be modest even with the less great because those who think politically are, like everyone else, embarked on the common search to shape man's destiny. However authoritarian and elitist a political thinker may be, he has to recognize that everyone has to have control over his life and death. And politics is the means, within nations and between them, of directing man's destiny.

Hobbes stated that the sovereign could – and should – do all things, *except* that the fear for one's life justifiably (and he could have added inescapably) did set limits on the sovereign's actions. Historians can always say that dead leaders should have been more ruthless or more liberal, more peaceful or more aggressive; this does not, after all, engage them in *real* wars, in *real* deaths; only those who think politically have the awful burden of giving advice and building theories that might, directly or indirectly, entail the death of men.

Those who think politically have therefore to be modest because one can never be sure – *absolutely* sure – that there is no better way of running men's affairs. If one is not certain that other proposals might be equally successful, and if failure can actually impair the destiny of men, then one must scrutinize all aspects of the situation before making decisions. Yet there are major difficulties due to lack of knowledge, lack of understanding of motivations, and lack of grasp of the deepest interrelationships between all the parts of the political system. Not surprisingly, political scientists are sometimes accused of being 'conservative' – students of structures and of behaviour in particular. Analysis of the intricacies of micro-politics suggests that there might be great difficulties in replacing current practices by other practices, however unsatisfactory current practices may be from an ideal viewpoint.

This is why those who think politically, and those who think politically professionally over a long period in particular, are often more conservative than those who come to political thought intermittently, indirectly or casually. There is therefore a case for constant rejuvenation of the profession, as there is a case for the rejuvenation of any organization. On this, too, political scientists must be modest. They should not reject outsiders, first, because they cannot, since matters of life and death will always be felt to be too important to be entrusted to a small coterie of professionals; and second, because the dialogue between professionals and amateurs both forces professionals to remain alerted to public concerns and incites amateurs to be less sure or less arrogant about their potential achievements.

Modesty about facts (which are so numerous) and modesty about men (who are often the facts) are thus the basic canons of thinking politically. Can a strict comparison be drawn between

political thinking and scientific thinking? It is true that many
sciences have questioned periodically their basic approaches;
but because of their successes, they have never given real prominence to critical thought. It may be that physics has come to a
crossroads; it may be that economics is questioning some of its
foundations. But in both these sciences, as in other sciences, the
bulk of the criticism comes from outside the profession – and
indeed often from those who think politically. Growth may not
be a need for all societies; the exploration of matter may have
become so esoteric, or so costly, that there is little to be said for
further and deeper probes. But these questions are questions of
political thought, as they raise the general issue of goals which
mankind has to have. Thinking politically has therefore to go
beyond science often, by questioning other sciences as well as its
own self, but this, too, must be done with the utmost modesty.
Galileo was sure – in physics, not in politics. To be sure in politics
is too dangerous and too partial to lead more than to occasional
(although at time useful) leaps into the unknown. And political
thinkers can only be modest about such a mission.

II.   *Being aware of underlying relationships in the maze of events*
Political thinking begins with an awareness that some underlying relations link events. A political approach thus contrasts
sharply with an extreme 'existential' viewpoint: events are not
just events – they can be organized, they can be 'explained'. To
say that one cannot explain is usually to say that the type of
explanation which has so far been used is not sufficient and
needs to be replaced, unless it simply means that one is well
satisfied with the state of affairs. The real difficulty is with those
who think that the problem is simple, that no training is required to solve it – that, in the last resort, anyone with a mind
can in a very short time give to political thought a new and
better twist.

   That political explanations are simple is one of the delusions
which brings to political thought many outsiders who, armed
with their discipline (if they are economists, linguists, historians,
philosophers or physicists), with their common sense (if they are
businessmen) or with their feelings (if they are social workers or
just observers of the life around them), think that they can easily
find some relationships hitherto unexplored and thus

revolutionize an 'easy' discipline. But the facts are too numerous and too diffuse – scattered around the world and in man's history – to make such expectations at all realistic.

There are good reasons, on the contrary, why some facts are seen in a particular way, and why various sorting processes lead to the categorization of facts: thinking politically is about knowing the categories, recognizing their type and thus proceeding to relationships on the basis of what is likely – though not certain – to emerge. The word that should be used is 'significance': not significance in a mathematical and highly technical sense, but significance which indicates a change in behaviour in structures or in ideology. An isolated event – an election victory, a military coup, a new party programme – can too easily be linked with other developments when in fact it is not significant at all, or is significant in a different way. Election victories are often viewed as decisive breakthroughs, whereas they may only be short-term trends, mostly displaying 'pendulum' signs; critical elections are rare.[1] Military coups repeat themselves, but their significance may be more hidden than outsiders might think: a coup in Greece is more significant than a coup in Peru, as it is less expected in the former than in the latter country.

Thus the very complexity of events gives rise to the belief in a 'free-for-all' in political thinking, while those who practise the art are as yet not able to give quick recipes which would show easily what relationships are and what naïve views of untrained amateurs. This is not because those who think politically jealously try to hide, like medieval craftsmen, the secrets of the trade and the tools of the profession. The tools are known: they are comparison and classification, the study of cases and the collection of facts, the discussion of concepts and their internal logic. But the relationships are still not clearly known; there are trends, but also exceptions; one has to know the trends to be able to perceive what is significant, but this process needs much monitoring and thus can only be told piecemeal and gradually. It would be an exaggeration – and perhaps immodest – to compare thinking politically to the aesthetic appreciation of

[1] See V. O. Key, 'A theory of critical elections' in *Journal of Politics* (February 17th, 1955), pp. 3-18, for an example of the reasons why some elections in the U.S., and only some elections, have been truly important.

the literary critic or the art collector; but the training, in part, is the same; fortunately or not, the rules cannot easily be specified; but no one who thinks politically can avoid the pressure to discover underlying patterns.

III.   *Being aware of the existence of distinct planes of analysis*

Two contradictory pitfalls have to be avoided in political thinking. First, the planes of analysis are linked, but distinct. Not all political scientists are sufficiently conscious of a divide between normative theory and descriptive analysis, or between the examination of behaviour and that of institutions. But, by and large, they know and have an instinct that many outsiders do not easily acquire. This instinct is one of the most obvious differences between politicians and those who think politically. Politicians are immersed in their own political life, in the moves of their colleagues: they naturally acquire a sense of which moves which are most likely, in the very short run, to give the desired results though of course they can err and make profound mistakes about their own futures.

But their view, as we said in Chapter 3, is conditioned by the structures in which they operate; they are accustomed to the modes of behaviour produced by these structures and may even derive, empirically, some 'laws' which will act as guides to future behaviour. Although they may sense that there is tension within these structures, because they find others dissatisfied about institutions or because they find themselves too narrowly constrained, they are unable to be 'objective' about the structures in which they operate. They rarely turn their thoughts to broader considerations, such as the likelihood of the structures breaking, or whether other structures would be acceptable. If they are truly 'alienated', and especially if the country has new institutions, they may propose reforms, even revolution. But this is a leap in the dark. And the leap in the dark is even more manifest when political leaders discuss and make suggestions for political change in countries outside their own, particularly in countries whose culture is very different from that which they know well. The more a political leader knows his own country and the more successful he is in understanding and affecting behaviour in his own national context, the more difficult it is for him to understand and affect behaviour where the political culture is very different. Many major mistakes – of American leaders with respect to the rest of the world, for instance – have stemmed from an inability to go beyond the familiar context of political life. Only if we recognize the profound differences that institutions, rules and arrangements produce can we begin to move towards an understanding of political life.

So it is not surprising that the world of political science is divided into normative theorists (at times dabbling in descriptive theory, but wanting to make their mark by analysing goals), behavioural theorists (at times also being concerned with lessons, but often criticized for being too narrow) and structural theorists (perhaps over-anxious to explain behaviour, yet soon recognizing the immense complexity of day-to-day action). The tools of all political scientists have many common features, but they are put to different uses; the diverse heritage of the various schools gives a different shape to the processes of thought. These distinctions must be seen. This is another reason for humility: by recognizing the diversity of the planes and of the types of thought implied, those who think politically are prepared to accept that new experiments have first to be examined within the precise context of one of the branches of the analysis.

IV.   *Being aware of links between the branches of political analysis*
Yet those who think politically have also to be aware of the important links that relate norms to structure and behaviour. Some new goals are perhaps not attainable, because institutions simply cannot bend to their demands or because behaviour remains too closely associated with the previous pattern of goals. Unless we are aware that there are relationships, though we may not know precisely what these relationships are, the analysis conducted within even one branch of political life will lack real foundations. Even utopias, as we saw, have to have some bearing on the reality as it is perceived by the political thinker and by the politicians and public whom he wants to convince; it is not very helpful to press for institutions which simply do not correspond to the broad pattern of goals which are commonly agreed to in a community; and patterns of behaviour need to be related to the framework of procedures and of institutions which happens to exist in a given system.

Changes in the system imply a modification of the

equilibrium of goals, structures, and behaviour which hitherto prevailed. This does not mean that changes cannot be implemented, nor that political thinkers should not be concerned with the type of changes which might bring the system nearer to what they feel to be a better way of organizing politics. But it does mean that, on balance, revolutionary changes are likely to be less frequent than is often claimed by those who are anxious to reform radically the political system which they see around them; and it means that changes will also have less effect, be slower, and take a more tortuous line than is often envisaged by those who come to embark on a revolutionary plan. To think politically means to accept that there are constraints, not only in everyday life, and within a given pattern of structures and behaviour, but in general, among all 'possible' patterns of norms, structures and behaviour which could be invented by imaginative thinkers.

V. *Being aware of continuous and discrete elements in political life*
The superposition of continuous and discrete elements of political life is perhaps the most baffling puzzle of political thinking. There are clear-cut 'models' which seem to present 'alternative' views of what society should be. There are clear-cut institutions, which can be defined and described. As we often noted, the political landscape is composed of a series of features which impose shape on the flow of behaviour. These features consist in certain configurations of structures, imposed or natural, due to history or suddenly arranged, which create habits and communication patterns and truly mould behaviour at the micro-level. There are, then, elements that are discrete, and have to be analysed as discrete elements; they may be analysed historically, with a careful description of their evolution. But they are solid features of the landscape and their disappearance creates a new set-up which needs to be explained in a different way.

Yet those who think politically must constantly beware of putting too much stress on discrete variations, as much of their experience is of continuous flow and of continuous change in both the behaviour and the strength of structures with which they are grappling. We noted the difficulty experienced by those who analyse behaviour in trying to measure these continuous flows, while seeing that the acceptance of structures could be compared with economics in terms of capital, except that a unit by which to measure this flow was not at the disposal of political thinkers.

The difficulty relates to some of the deeper aspects of the many mysteries of political life. To think politically is to be able to see where there is a trend, or a break, in a pattern, be it of elections, or of a party system, or of democracy in a country. But to think politically is also to think of alternatives, not only in patterns of structures embodying various norms, but at the level of decision-making and decision processes. Some processes may be 'incremental'; but not all are: breaks in decision patterns seem frequently to occur. We saw that it was difficult, if we looked at the problem in detail, to define precisely what a decision was. At the other extreme, it is as difficult to be sure about goals, about the relationship between various goals, and thus about the point where one goal is sought instead of another. We are never certain of what is continuous and of what is a break in our own life, in our feelings, in our behaviour patterns: those who think politically are naturally even more cautious when they come to distinguish between continuous and discrete elements in the political life of a community.

One could find – we did find – many similarities between thinking politically and the types of thinking which are to be observed in other sciences. As we already said, the purpose here is not to establish whether political thinking is a 'science' or not. Perhaps political thinking is less rigorous than scientific thinking, although the problems faced by economists, chemists or physicists may simply be less complex and intricate than the problems posed by political life. Political thinking has to be related, not to scientific thinking in other disciplines, but to the object of study of political analysis.

At times, those who think politically deplore the fact that their discipline is so broad that, despite all efforts, it never seems to reach the calmer shores where harmony, continuous development and elegant laws clarify the problems of study. But man is not simple, calm and harmonious; which is why a political thinker is sceptical of any explanation that demands more harmony of man than he possesses. Thinking politically is a hazardous process – it attracts adventurers and poets, as well as 'hard' men, just as politics attracts dreamers and 'hard' men, realists and idealists. They all have to be understood and accounted for if thinking politically is to be both a record of man's actions and a guide to man's future.

Selected bibliography

A comprehensive bibliography would extend over the total output of political science throughout the ages, since the subject of this book is the profession of political science. The bibliography which is listed here is thus only a very tiny fraction of what a comprehensive bibliography would constitute. Apart from some of the great classics, more general studies are included which give an idea of the different types of approaches in normative, behavioural and structural theories that characterize modern political science; cases and case-studies are not listed, though, together, they constitute an important approach. They are so numerous and the subject-matter so diverse that they would be confusing in so short a book. Readers can refer to the bibliographies of some of the general works corresponding to each approach if they wish to see how detailed studies, which constitute the bulk of the daily production of political science, are conducted. Many of the ideas and approaches which characterize cases and case-studies are represented in some of the general works that are listed below.

I. Great classics

Aristotle, *Politics* (Heinemann, London, 1932)
Bagehot, *The English Constitution* (Oxford University Press, 1928)
Burke, *Reflections on the Revolution in France* (Holt, Rinehart & Winston, New York, 1959)
Cooper, *The American Democrat* (Penguin Books, Harmondsworth, 1969)
Hobbes, *Leviathan* (Basil Blackwell, Oxford, 1946)
Locke, *Two Treatises of Civil Government* (Dent, London, 1924)
Machiavelli, *The Prince* (Dent, London, 1968)
Hamilton, et al, *The Federalist* (Dent, London, 1948)
Marx, *Captial* (Allen & Unwin, London, 1946)
Mill, *Representative Government* (Oxford University Press, 1912)
—*On Liberty* (Oxford University Press, 1912)
Montesquieu, *The Spirit of Laws* (J. Nourse & P. Vaillant, London, 1750)
More, *Utopia* (Macmillan, London, 1908)
Paine, *The Rights of Man* (Dent, London, 1954)
Plato, *The Republic* (Cambridge University Press, 1963)
Rousseau, *The Social Contract* (Dent, London and Toronto, 1973)
Tocqueville, *Democracy in America* (Oxford University Press, 1946)

160   Thinking Politically

II. General

Cowling, H., *Nature and Limits of Political Science* (Cambridge University Press, 1963)
Dahl, R. A., *Modern Political Analysis* (Prentice-Hall, New York, 1963)
Duverger, M., *The Idea of Politics* (Methuen, London, 1966)
Easton, D., *Varieties of Political Theory* (Prentice-Hall, New York, 1966)
Miller, J. D. B., *The Nature of Politics* (Duckworth, London, 1962)
Popper, K., *The Open Society and its Enemies* (Routledge and Kegan Paul, London, 1945)
Spitz., D., *Political Theory and Social Change* (Athlone Press, New York, 1957)
Strickland, D. A., L. L. Wade and R. E. Johnston, *A Primer of Political Analysis* (Markham, Chicago, 1968)
Winch, P., *The Idea of a Social Science* (Routledge & Kegan Paul, London, 1958)
Young, R. ed., *Approaches to the Study of Politics* (Northwestern University Press, Evanston, 1958)

III. Normative theory

Arblaster, A., and S. Lukes, *The Good Society* (Methuen, London, 1971)
Bachrach, P., *The Theory of Democratic Elitism* (University of London Press, 1969)
Barry, B., *Political Argument* (Routledge & Kegan Paul, London, 1963)
—*Sociologists, Economists and Democracy* (Macmillan, London, 1970)
Benn, S. I., and R. S. Peters, *Social Principles and the Democratic State* (Allen & Unwin, London, 1959)
Mannheim, K., *Ideology and Utopia* (Routledge & Kegan Paul, London, 1966)
Marcuse, H., *One-dimensional Man* (Routledge & Kegan Paul, London, 1964)
Meehan, E. J., *Contemporary Political Thought* (Dorsey Press, London, 1967)
Oakeshott, M. *Rationalism in Politics* (Methuen, London, 1962)
Plamenatz, J., *Consent, Freedom and Political Obligation* (Oxford University Press, 1968)
Sabine, G. H., *History of Political Theory* (Garrap, London, 1963)
Sibley, M. Q., *Political Ideas and Ideologies* (Harper & Row, New York, 1970)
Strauss, L., *What is Political Philosophy?* (Free Press, New York, 1959)
Strauss, L. and J. Coopsey, *History of Political Philosophy* (Rand McNally, Chicago, 1963)
Weldon, T. D., *The Vocabulary of Politics* (Penguin Books, Harmondsworth, 1953)

IV. Behavioural theory

Alker, H., *Mathematics and Politics* (Macmillan, London, 1965)
Black, D., *The Theory of Committees and Elections* (Cambridge University Press, London, 1958)
Buchanan, J. M. and G. Tullock, *The Calculus of Consent* (University of Michigan Press, 1962)
Curry, R. L., and L. L. Wade, *A Theory of Political Exchange* (Prentice-Hall, New York, 1968)

Deutsch, K. W., *The Nerves of Government* (Free Press, New York, 1963)

Downs, A., *An Economic Theory of Democracy* (Harper & Row, New York, 1957)

Nicholson, M., *Conflict Analysis* (English University Press, London, 1970)

Olson, M., Jr., *The Logic of Collective Action* (Harvard University Press, Cambridge, Mass., 1965)

Ranney, A. ed., *Essays on the Behavioural Study of Politics* (University of Illinois Press, Illinois, 1962)

Smelser, N., *A Theory of Collective Behaviour* (Routledge & Kegan Paul, London, 1962)

Tullock, G., *Towards a Mathematics of Politics* (University of Michigan Press, Michigan, 1967)

Ulmer, S., ed., *Introductory Readings in Political Behaviour* (Rand McNally, Chicago, 1961)

V. Structural theory

Almond, G. A., and T. S. Coleman, *The Politics of the Developing Areas* (Princeton University Press, Princeton, 1960)

Almond, G. A., and G. B. Powell, *Comparative Politics* (Little, Brown, Bosch, Boston, 1966)

Apter, D., *Choice and the Politics of Allocation* (Yale University Press, 1971)

—*The Politics of Modernization* (University of Chicago Press, 1965)

Blondel, J., *Introduction to Comparative Government* (Praeger, New York, 1970)

Dahl, R. A., *Polyarchy* (Yale University Press, Yale, 1971)

Easton, D., *The Political System* (Knopf, New York, 1953)

—*A Systems Analysis of Political Life* (Wiley, New York, 1965)

Merton, R., *Social Theory and Social Structure* (Free Press, New York, 1968)

Index